TAKE BACK YOUR WEALTH

Moving from **Lack** to *Abundance*

"*This book is a game changer!*"
— Dr. George C. Fraser

RODNEY D. ARCHER
IN PARTNERSHIP WITH FAMILY WEALTH COMMUNITY

This book is dedicated to our growing wealth building communities nationwide.

CHEERS TO YOUR FIVE STAR SUCCESS LIVING!

Your Family Wealth Representative

"The thief comes only in order to steal, kill, and destroy. I came that they may have and enjoy life, and have it in abundance."

John 10:10 AMP

Contents

ENLIGHTENMENT

INTRODUCTION 6
PREPARATION FOR FIVE STAR SUCCESS......................................14
    You Are Here For A Greater Purpose 16
    It Is Time To Become Strategic 18
    Get Re-Conditioned To Act Like A Winner 28
    Questions For Review & Reflection: 32
PRELUDE TO FIVE STAR SUCCESS.. 34
    There Are Timeless Practices 36
    There Are Business Best Practices 56
    Systems Of Domination 60
    Questions For Review & Reflection: 86
PURSUIT OF FIVE STAR SUCCESS..88
    Gaining Key Money Skill Sets 90
    Questions For Review & Reflection: 148
PROSPERITY OF FIVE STAR SUCCESS 150
    Building A Prosperous Community 152
    Changing Our World 156
    Early Disciplines 162
    The Educator, Coach & Guide 166
    Buy And Build Wealth 170
    Lifetime & Legacy Wealth 174
    Questions For Review & Reflection: 178
POSTERITY OF FIVE STAR SUCCESS..180
    Transform To Greater For Preservation 182
    Protect & Preserve Assets Forever 182
    The Conclusive Summary 200
    Questions For Review & Reflection: 204
ACKNOWLEDGEMENTS 208
RESOURCES 210
AUTHOR & COMMUNITY 217

Contents

ENGAGEMENT

CHAPTER 1	PREPARATION FOR FIVE STAR SUCCESS	14
	True Identity	17
	Reading Is Fundamental	19
	Delayed Gratification	21
	The Money Love Letter	23
	The Art Of War And Money	31
CHAPTER 2	PRELUDE TO FIVE STAR SUCCESS	34
	The Rules About Money	39
	Quality Service, Delivery, & Following	59
	Understanding Money Systems	65
	Spreading The Good News	85
	The Iconic Story	87
CHAPTER 3	PURSUIT OF FIVE STAR SUCCESS	88
	Destination: Five Star Success	107
	Young And Strategic	113
	It Is What You Keep That Matters	117
	Making Moves, Feeling Good	123
	Being An Owner & Wealth Builder	129
	Leaders Must Make Sacrifices	133
	Being Intentional With Every Move	145
CHAPTER 4	PROSPERITY OF FIVE STAR SUCCESS	150
	Achieving More, Living Better	155
	Adventures Of Kimbellman	165
	New Possibilities	173
CHAPTER 5	POSTERITY OF FIVE STAR SUCCESS	180
	Family Business & Trust Affairs	183
	Law Of The Lid	187
	Time & Progress	195
ACKNOWLEDGEMENTS		208
RESOURCES		210
AUTHOR & COMMUNITY		217

INTRODUCTION

After years of working with people and families, I saw how fragmented our society was, each person trying desperately to figure out how they were going to make ends meet, SURVIVE, and how they were going to have a decent quality of life in the future.

The same people worried how their children were going to make out in the rapidly changing information and technology world if no better information or skill sets were introduced to them, what would their quality of life be like?

This book is for those who feel that you have been left behind or are left in bewilderment of how you got where you are, being far behind the plans you had for yourself and the goals you sought to accomplish.

This book is a blueprint (Left Side Pages) of how you can turn your life around financially, starting with knowing about the systems that exist and how to counter the systems for your greater benefit. It also shows an example of a community (Right Side Pages) of people just like you who got fed up with status quo and began to make sacrifices of time and adjustments to their thinking and lifestyle to break the curse of lack off of their own lives and build a better foundation for their children and grandchildren to build upon.

It is my desire that you learn about the principles, rules, tools, and strategies to gain financial control of your life, so you may live life on your own terms; owning your time, your money, your good name, and leaving a worthwhile legacy for generations to prosper from.

It is time you balance the conversation with knowledge and understanding, income and wealth, finance and business, today and tomorrow so you may be fully aware that both are equally important for a financially secure and rewarding life. Neglecting one for the other can no longer be an option.

Throughout the book, you will see a hand show up to emphasize STOP and pay attention to five points that will be made and what they mean. Share your knowledge with friends, family, co-workers, etc. This will help you internalize the information being shared.

You will see the following, not necessarily in the order you see them here:

Five Money Systems   **Five Money Rules**
Five Strategies of War   **Five Tax Advantage Strategies**
Five Star Success Company   **Five Passive Income Methods**
Five Asset Classes   **Five P's For Business Development**
Five Star Success   **Five Star Service Survey Questions**
Five Target Organizations   **Five Layers of Financial Portfolio**
Five Routine Practices   **Five Practices As Code Breaker**
Five Effects On Credit   **Five Ways To Acquire A Home**
Five Tiers to Building Business Credit

There will be a lot of other pertinent information shared also, just don't memorize info for trivia purposes but let it transform your life, so you may be an example for others to follow.

This is a modern-day exodus, leading the masses from economic bondage to financial freedom, leading the families from division to cohesiveness, and leading various communities from lack to abundance.

This is done by having a clear and distinct vision for each person to obtain. It sets the basis of skill set mastery to be able to build a financial empire on. There are elementary steps and building blocks for everything and so must be the case regarding personal finance and business development.

It is my pleasure to work with our template community in Charlotte, NC, a group of people with a true collaborative mindset and a spirit to help others succeed as themselves. We are Family Wealth, "Strategies for Financial Success." We hope you join us in our vision to change the financial landscape for millions of Americans.

The Lack Dilemma

There is an economic dilemma where the statistics are steadily getting worse as we witness retailers like Sears, Kmart, Radio Shack, HH Gregg and numerous others go out of business. We have seen manufacturers relocate for cheaper labor in neighboring countries like Rexnord Corporation, which makes industrial bearings headquartered in Indianapolis, move to Mexico (to pay workers $3 per hour with no benefits versus $25 per hour and benefits) or corporations outsource customer service to foreign countries. Furthermore, people in the service-oriented industries, i.e. food industry, hospitality industry, and manufacturing industry are being replaced with robotics and artificial intelligence. It sounds like a sci-fi movie...doesn't it?

This major shift in the marketplace has people scrambling to find answers. More people are working two to three jobs per person or working as much overtime as they can to keep up but still seem to be falling further behind in debt and though they desire to retire, they cannot see a viable solution.

Those who have steady income working for corporate America or a branch of government are, as a majority, having to work until they die. This is due to not having a financial education and only having an academic education. Both educations are required.

"An Academic Education Is For Earning A Living, A Financial Education Is For Building Lifetime and Legacy Wealth." —Rodney Archer

This book caters to the hard working Middle Class that is steadily sliding downward, working harder but accomplishing less and less in regards to building lasting wealth for retirement and heirs to build upon.

In response to the shifting of jobs and the reduction of labor, more people are attempting to start small businesses. Unfortunately, most have very little experience, no conditioning for the mental toughness required, minimal interpersonal skills to attract and retain good talent, and finally, very little capital necessary to build the business to scale and to last. So they gamble their 401(k)s, savings, and rack up credit card debt in hopes that it will all work out. The older everyone gets, the more desperate they become. Many also turn to real estate with no experience or seasoning in a commission-only or investing environment. They often consume valuable time and more money they can't afford to lose.

Therefore, lack, which is the limitation of resources whether we are speaking of a steady, frequent, and sufficient stream of income or sufficient capital to undergird businesses are becoming more prevalent. Furthermore, our lifetime accumulation of wealth is grossly negligent in comparison to the amount of debt that is left for the succeeding generations. Or perhaps lack refers to lacking disclosure of information for comparison purposes.

How did lack occur?

The beginning of lack can be traced back to 1971, when currency was no longer backed by gold (though initiated in 1933). Without the gold standard, government spending began to exponentially increase and the government debt also devalued the purchasing power of the dollar. The declining purchasing power is called inflation (or a higher cost of goods) and hidden taxation which affects every American citizen. So based on the purchasing power of $100 in 1971, the equivalent at the end of 2017 was $604 (a 504% increase) which averages 3.99% a year in inflation over 46 years. Compare this to practically no inflation (20% increase) for 238 years from 1775 to 1913. Over the years, the government spending has included creating larger government regulating departments for entitlement or subsidy programs around Social Security, Food Stamps, Unemployment Insurance, Disability Insurance, Medicare, Medicaid, Housing Subsidies, Education Subsidies, etc. Over half of the 318 million American population is dependent on the government for benefits.

Also, if wages are not keeping up with price increases in the areas of housing (6.4% average yearly increase from 1968 to 2004) and education (7.64% average yearly increase from 1980 to 2014 for college tuition), then it causes people to work more hours or more jobs to make ends meet. The wages in comparison have increased on average 6.21% per year from 1960 to 2018. Social Security cost of living adjustments (COLA) have averaged 3.02% from 1984 to 2006 with little to no increases in 2009, 2010, 2015, and 2016. Medicare Part B (Insurance Premiums) and Part D (Drug Premium) increases also negates any cost of living increases as well.

As a summary, if wages are not keeping up with inflation and senior benefits are even less than what is required for sustaining a quality of life during elder years, we have a crisis on our hands. All of these facts require the American people to become more productive by creating more businesses, accumulating more capital, generating more income, and becoming more financially savvy with financial savings and investments in order to have surplus.

Another cause of lack occurred after ERISA (Employment Retirement Income Security Act) was enacted in 1974. ERISA was designed to protect employees from the mishandling of their retirement funds from Pension Fund Managers. The Defined Benefit plans were true pensions set up by employers on employees' behalf for a stress-free retirement. In the 1980s, corporations began to navigate away from Defined Benefit Plans and started offering Defined Contribution Plans like 401(k)s where the contribution and growth became the sole responsibility of the employee with no financial education or training.

By 1990 both plans were in the marketplace equally with pensions declining rapidly and 401(k)s increasing rapidly. In 2013, Vanguard reported a median savings for ages 55 to 64 being only $76,381. The Social Security website showed a life expectancy for a man to be 84.3 years old and 86.5 years old for women. If relying on social security and the pittance for retirement savings, it is no wonder why 95% of Americans are broke or still working at the age of 65.

We have listed at least two specific examples of when the lack started over 40 years ago, but the bottom line is three-fold:

1) People are not given full disclosure of choices and alternatives to traditional financial vehicles.

2) People are not receiving financial education to understand the money and wealth rules.

3) People are not receiving entrepreneurial education to understand how to establish and build a business as a system and to scale to generate more income.

The Solution

TAKE BACK Your Wealth lays out a blueprint starting with concepts and simple money systems to understand what is causing lack, then introduce a mindset paradigm shift to take back what is rightfully ours, which is our lives and our wealth. We then share proven strategies to improve or create income streams as well as build lifetime and legacy wealth.

TAKE BACK Your Wealth is like having two books in one as one aspect is informational and instructional and the other tells fictional stories, inspired by real members of Family Wealth.

We introduce Family Wealth as a wealth building community who is coming together, learning together, working together, and building wealthy families together. This is done by each person being an inspiration for others and each person having accountability from their family or community to transform the information into habits, then desired results.

Our Group Learning Strategy

In order to condense time frames for learning and reconditioning the mindset to adopt new habits, we believe the economic dilemma can only be confronted in a community environment. A community consists of people who are tired of the rat race and desire a greater quality of life, without the long hours and long years of working. The community must have:

1) Commonality (like minded, similar objective)
2) Communication (learn, share, repeat)
3) Commune (fellowship and social interaction)
4) Commerce (buy and sell in trade with each other)

As a community of wealth builders being built throughout the U.S., they can connect to churches, corporations, non-profit organizations, etc. Family Wealth is a community of like-minded individuals addressing our financial dilemma, going from lack to abundance.

We endeavor to equip leaders of a community with the essential information to empower families and groups of people in various parts of the country representing numerous ethnic groups as well. There are four roles to ensure ongoing sharing and training in the community.

1) Wealth Ambassador (Financial Educator & Community Connector)
2) Wealth Strategist (Introduces Financial Tools & Strategies)
3) Business Strategist (Business Coach & Guide)
4) Wealth Builder (A Customer & Example)

As a community, we are leading everyone toward mastering five money skill sets, which we call Five Star Success. These skill sets are a countermeasure to the Money Systems that extract time, labor, and resources from the average American citizen. Such methods are how you will go from lack to abundance.

Five Star Success Living consists of the mastery of:

★ Creating Passive Income $24K + Per Year

★ Achieving 700 + Credit Scores

★ Acquiring and Owning Real Estate

★ Obtaining Debt Freedom In Ten years Or Less

★ Building Equity In Assets Of $200K +

Get ready for the time of your life. Learn the money game! Get out of the rat race, the slave-servant existence, and live life at a greater fulfilling level.

It is our intent to elevate you, the reader from a consumer to a merchant, from a debtor to an owner, and from a laborer to a wealth builder.

- Rodney D. Archer

Let's get started...

CHAPTER # ONE

PREPARATION FOR FIVE STAR SUCCESS

FAMILY WEALTH COMMUNITY
ENGAGEMENT OF CONCEPTS

—$ **TAKE BACK YOUR WEALTH!** $—

YOU ARE HERE FOR A GREATER PURPOSE

As a consumer, we earn money and spend money via cash or credit. We pacify ourselves and justify buying things we don't need with money we don't have to impress people we don't like to still feel unfulfilled and insignificant in the world.

So as the world turns, we live paycheck to paycheck, chasing money, positions, and titles to gain more stuff as we fill our calendars with more activities. Our passion and our purpose gets less attention. It feels like we have been in a constant mode of survival just to stay alive, just to keep food on the table, the lights and gas on, etc. And we wonder if things will get better? Or is this as good as it gets?

There are the degrees from college, driving the nice cars, having the nice home, the charter schools for the children, the four-week vacations, the Y memberships, the 401(k), the 529 plans and Gerber plans. Even though there are the outer appearances of doing well and being successful, something is still not right.

There are the social club affiliations, the church or temple memberships, the giving of tithes, volunteering time with charities, serving as Board of Director, volunteering with Parent Teacher Association, attending HOA meetings, etc.

Yet, what is missing? What is wrong? Why, despite all of the activity, nothing seems to be getting accomplished?

Could it be because we have been marginalized to being a consumer vs. a merchant, a debtor vs. an owner and a laborer vs. a wealth builder? Are those words similar to how we should be the head, not the tail, the lender, not the borrower? Sounds familiar?

The opposite of what we should represent has become the long-standing reality. This is why there is so much lack vs. abundance.

— Moving from Lack to *Abundance* —

TRUE IDENTITY

The story consists of the Family Wealth community who meet on the 16th floor conference room in downtown Charlotte, NC. A weekly empowerment series takes place with teaching and sharing financial principles and strategies. The lives of everyone involved are very busy trying to balance work, a side business, family, school, children's activities, etc. Members of the community still make the sacrifices to meet up as often as possible because they gain inspiration from their peers to stay the course with their plan to achieve Five Star Success. Let's join them in their weekly meeting.

Pastor Sean: How's everything? Thanks for coming out. We are so glad that you joined us this evening. I am personally elated to see the growth of everyone as you mature in the areas of finance and business. Amen.

Kimbell: Me too.

Pastor Sean: Please tell me what progress you have made that you are proud of. Let's go around the room.

Marques: I guess I'll go first. I have to say my mindset has been the most affected over these last few months since I joined the Family Wealth Community. I am learning the difference between being a debtor vs. owner and a consumer vs. wealth builder. Who I perceive myself to be, makes a huge difference on how I act, which ultimately affects my reality. The saying is true, *"Change your mindset, you change your habits. If you change your habits, you can change your life."* I had been in survival mode for so long, knowing I needed to be saving but as soon as I earn the money, I'm spending it on a good time hanging out with my friends over the weekend or always dealing with some kind of emergency. I had to admit that I had been conditioned to being a spender and not a saver and furthermore living off of credit cards haven't helped much.

—$ **TAKE BACK YOUR WEALTH!** $—

IT IS TIME TO BECOME STRATEGIC

"...If you do not obey...and carefully follow...commands and decrees... they will lend to you, but you will not lend to them. They will be the head but you will be the tail." - Deuteronomy 28: 15,44

YOU ARE A CREATOR, an innovator, a contributor back to the world first and foremost. Your time, effort, and resources have been taken hostage so that you have no time but to repeat the same cycle of a mere existence every day. There is more!

YOU ARE AN OWNER. You should Own Your Time, Own Your Name, Own Your Finances, Own Your Wealth, Own Your Legacy and yet all has been given to someone else to control and manage. Take your rightful place!

YOU ARE A WEALTH BUILDER. *"A good man (or woman) leaves an inheritance for his (or her) children's children."* Isn't it only right that after living 70+ years that something of value should be passed down to the generations that follow to build upon? Should they have to start with debt and labor all of their lives to repeat the cycle you and I created?

Shouldn't the change, shouldn't the curse of lack be broken? And shouldn't it start with you and I, right here, right now, in this dispensation of time?

Okay warrior, if you are in agreement, let's get our battle plan together so we may forge ahead for our victory and the prosperity of our heirs.

✋ There are at least **Five Strategies in the Art of War or Chess** and they are as follows:

    1) Know The Rules Of Engagement

    2) Know Your Opponent & Yourself

    3) Capitalize On Time

    4) Be Patient With Your Own Plan

— Moving from Lack to *Abundance* —

"GENERAL:" Marques, you're admitting that you have been living in survival mode is very important to realize, like an alcoholic admitting that they are an alcoholic. That is the first step. What has helped you think more as the wealth builder vs. consumer or owner vs. debtor?

Marques: I think what helped me to turn my financial perspective around was knowing that there is a three in one system made of the government, corporations, and banks who treat me like a game piece on a Monopoly board, extracting money and wealth from me at every opportunity. I am fed up with feeding and funding someone else's riches and luxury coffers vs. my own. I knew I had to see myself as deserving better in life so I looked at myself in the mirror to honestly evaluate who I was. Once I decided I was going to be the owner and not the borrower, I had to take charge of my financial life. I feel much better about where I am heading financially.

Pastor Sean: That is awesome! I can tell that there is much that you're thankful for. Amen. Who else would like to share? What progress have you made and are proud of?

READING IS FUNDAMENTAL

Shaughn Lee: I am glad to be reading more to stimulate my mind, from personal development books and audiobooks like Zig Ziglar's See You At The Top or Over The Top or Brian Tracy's No Excuses and reading the classics on personal finance like Think & Grow Rich by Napoleon Hill or The Richest Man In Babylon by George Clason and others. What caught my attention was the amount of TV watching or unproductive busyness I can find myself doing. I tell myself I am so busy with working all day, tutoring my two sons, doing my business thing, and catering to my wife, all I want to do is rest and watch TV or check out what is going on with social media. I became awakened to the fact that living vicariously

5) Be Willing To Make All Sacrifices

Rules Of Engagement

There is a cycle that has been created for the benefit of the Three in One System made up of the Government, Corporations, and Banks. The system is excellent at extracting time, energy, and resources from the consumer, the borrower, and laborer.

Each member of the system has an expertise. The government specializes in cash flow via tax revenues. The corporation specializes in equity distribution or shares among its shareholders and the banks specialize in leverage of cash deposits for lending purposes.

See the diagram below, how it works and how you fit as a game piece being moved around the cycle system.

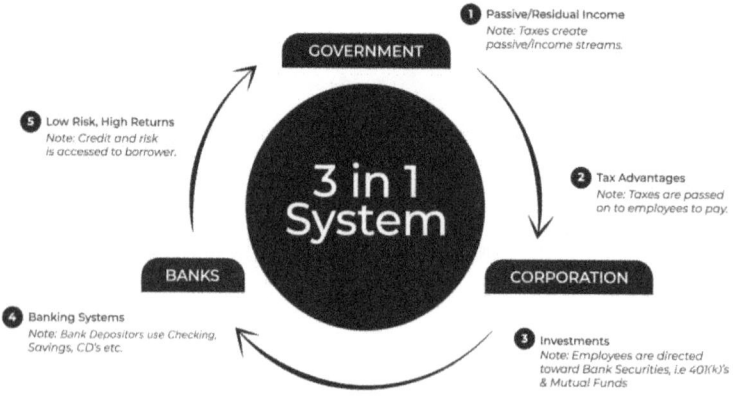

through reality shows and peering in on other people's lives was not helping me, progress toward the quality of life I desired for myself and family. When I found out that the poor have big TV's and the rich and wealthy have big libraries, it was enough for me to invest in audio books and books to keep expanding my mind to greater possibilities. Aviance and I share conversations around what we are reading, and it helps our relationship, being on one accord with where we are heading as a couple. We read or listen in the course of the day and during the evening we shut everything down to talk about what each of us learned on that given day.

Aviance: You know the saying, those who read together stay together.

"GENERAL:" Well maybe I'll try that next time since nothing else worked in my last two marriages (chuckle).

Pastor Sean: Readers are leaders and leaders are readers. All of the secrets are hidden in books that most people don't bother to read, including the Bible for that matter. Amen.

Tani: Let me go next, Pastor Sean.

Pastor Sean: Sure Tani, please share.

DELAYED GRATIFICATION

Tani: I am most proud of delayed gratification, just being more patient with my financial plan and not justifying buying shoes, furniture, going on trips, etc. at a whim. The idea of not deserving it until I can pay for it immediately or within thirty days was very hard for me. I was a shopaholic and a credit card addict. I would find something to spend the card on to max it out. My credit scores were horrible as a result. Can you imagine me having 500 or so credit scores? (Everybody in the room nodded yes, they could see her having 500 or so scores

—$ TAKE BACK YOUR *W*EALTH! $—

1) The Government collects tax revenue from its citizens. This produces cash flow for the government.

2) State Government gives tax advantages to corporations and the tax liability is passed on to the employees.

3) Employees are directed toward bank securities, i.e. mutual funds, index funds, inside 401(k)s, 403(b)s, etc. This produces fees for the Investment Banking Industry.

4) Bank depositors are encouraged to use CD's, money market accounts, checking and saving accounts. Savings serve as reserves for bank leveraging.

5) Banks access risks for lending purposes via mortgages, car notes, credit cards, business loans, etc. The bank builds assets from those who borrow.

Note: From bank profits, banks purchase Government Bonds for the government to pay its bills. This completes the cycle.

The bank is the biggest player in the Three in One System with the investment or security instruments, where money is made on the trades, commercial banking where cash deposits are leveraged as Reserves, and profits from interest earned on lending.

DO WHAT THE BANKS DO, NOT WHAT THEY SAY. You must imitate the Three in One System for your own advantage vs. feeding into the system. The way to counter the Three in One System is to master the Five Money Systems it uses, which are Credit, Cash Flow, Business, Banking and Investments. We will cover this information a little later.

Know Your Opponent

"If you know your enemy and yourself, you need not fear the results of a hundred battles." —Sun Tzu

Your opponent is made up of four forces that seek to come against your money and they are **D.I.R.T.**

Debt—The more debt, the more bondage, the more hours worked, and

Moving from Lack to *Abundance*

since she is always flaunting the latest brand and talking about how she got her fourth Coach purse on sale for $299 vs. $450 while making roughly $55K a year in salary). The only way I could cure my addiction was to cut up the majority of my credit cards and use debit cards or cash only. I have found out that life goes on without them and by using my debit cards or cash only, I either have it in my bank account to spend or I don't. If I don't and I want it bad enough, I save up to get it so I can own it free and clear. I have been credit card, shopaholic free for eight months now.

Pastor Sean: That is wonderful! Being less dependent on credit and having more self-discipline is a lesson for all of us in the room. Amen.

"GENERAL:" Breaking the consumer mentality and debt consciousness is a worthwhile accomplishment for any of us. One thing I have learned is that, being a consumer and debtor leaves us in a constant state of lack, just enough, living paycheck to paycheck and wondering why we can't get ahead. If we focus rather on being an owner and wealth builder like Marques suggested, our actions will follow. Another way of saying it is owning and controlling, Nelson Rockefeller is known for saying *"Control everything and own nothing."* I agree, yet we have to own it in order to control it. The reality is that we all desire to own our time, own our money (resources), and be able to pursue our dreams and goals with plenty of resources to do so. How we think is like the bit in the mouth of a horse, its direction determines its destination.

Pastor Sean: This was a great session, we have learned much about having an owner and wealth building mindset. Thanks for sharing. Let's reconvene next week. Amen.

THE MONEY LOVE LETTER

The community dismisses, fellowships and networks with newcomers at

the less wealth is being built.

Inflation—The higher the cost of goods, the less purchasing power there is. The saver becomes the loser, because inflation outpaces saving rates.

Retirement—The retirement vehicles are deceptive with fees, risk of loss, and heavy with restrictions and penalties.

Taxes—Various forms of taxes are lashed at the common man and woman, without corporations, trusts, and property.

To defeat the four forces and rise above D.I.R.T, that which causes lack, it requires eliminating debt quickly, outpacing inflation, using the most effective retirement vehicles with less fees, more growth, and the minimizing of taxes.

Know Yourself

YOU ARE A CREATOR. You are a merchant, one who packages your gifts, talents, and insights for distribution to the masses, for the betterment of mankind.

When you package up and distribute your gifts and talents to the masses, the world will be grateful for your contribution.

YOU ARE AN OWNER. You are one who takes responsibility for your life and your results in life this far. You will control all that you gain ownership of.

YOU ARE A WEALTH BUILDER. Your life's mission is to multiply what you have been given, to outwit your adversary and produce a harvest in your lifetime. You will defeat the enemy of lack, so your heirs may walk in prosperity.

empowerment event. In between weeks, the members deal with their various life episodes.

Pastor Sean: Kim baby, where did this bill come from? A medical bill? First, the electric bill went up and then the HOA for the home. Why does it seem as fast as the money comes in, it leaves much faster? How can we ever prepare for retirement if we are always in survival mode, paying bills year after year? We give tithes and offerings and are thankful for all we have. Our needs are met yet there is more that is desired. What are we doing wrong?

Lady Kim: Remember when we went to Dr. Matt's Inspired Millionaire session and he told us how we have to be in alignment or congruent with our mind, will, and emotions? And if we are not, it creates a blockage in the flow of what we desire? He talked about how everything is energy, vibrations, and frequency. If deep in our subconscious, we believe there will only be just enough and never surplus then that is what we get over and over again. And I think it may be how we talk imposing some doubt like we say, *"If it be the Lord's will"* and *"Hopefully"* as though we don't fully believe what we ask the universe for. Or we will say, *"I don't want to be broke, or poor"* or that *"We are tired of just scraping by."* Those comments carry negative frequencies with them and according to the law of attraction, like attracts like. Honey, I say we, because I am just as guilty, but I know that you and I can speak more in the affirmative, be more thankful, more often and write our love letter to our money.

Pastor Sean: Love letter to our money?

Lady Kim: Yes, do you remember the exercise that Dr. Matt wanted us to do as a homework assignment?

Pastor Sean: Yes, I remember him saying it. It seemed kind of silly.

Lady Kim: Yes, and was it silly for Naaman to dip seven times in the Jordan river to be cleansed of leprosy? What do you think Mr. Bible Scholar?

—$ TAKE BACK YOUR *W*EALTH! $—

Capitalize On Time

Once time is spent, there is no do-over. You have one life. The past has gone and records the history of its moments. The future is in front of you and is open to the shaping and molding of its appearance. Now, the very present is a gift of time for immediate use. What is done and what is done most effectively makes all of the difference.

"Do not dwell in the past, do not dream of the future, concentrate the mind on the present." - Buddha

Regardless of where you are financially or how old you are, at the point of revelation, knowledge and inspiration, choose to act immediately. Think about your children and grandchildren, set them up early for financial success all throughout their lifetime, not just up till college.

"Money needs time to build wealth. Most Americans look at 20 years at a time, institutions look at 60 to 80 years at a time, we must change our paradigm for building wealth." - Rodney Archer

You will be given truth, tools, and strategies to turn your financial circumstances around. Remember information without application leads to stagnation.

Be Patient with Your Own Plan

It is said that in order for an apprentice (or student) to become a master, it requires 10,000 hours of study and practice. Ten thousand hours equate to seven to ten years.

Most people will not endeavor seven to ten years in any one direction. They will not FOCUS, thus Follow One Course Until Successful. When one is downloaded with ideas to change their financial dilemma or to change the world, is there such a thing as failure or is it just not enough effort given in the right manner over the necessary amount of time?

"Any target attacked with the right actions in the right amounts with persistence is attainable." - Grant Cardone

Moving from Lack to *Abundance*

Pastor Sean: Good point. Why oh why do you make so much sense? I believe you are right. There must be something out of alignment and I am willing to be obedient to the process to living an abundant life. Amen.

Lady Kim: Let's begin to write our love letter to our money. I'll help.

Dear Abundance,

This is Pastor Sean and Lady Kim, we haven't taken time to share our honest thoughts with you. Most of the time, we speak out of frustration of how you disappoint us. Just when we expect a breakthrough, the same ole result manifest…just enough. It has been a lackluster relationship, not really excited about having you in our life but only being a necessity to pay our bills and pay our tithes and offerings. It feels like we must please God and our electric and gas company, still we desire so much more for ourselves. We find ourselves going through the motions perhaps living a quiet depression on the inside but smiling and giving the impression all is well on the outside.

For any relationship to thrive, we realize that there must be open dialogue, honest communication so we apologize for taking our relationship for granted. We are ready to apply the Universal Laws in our favor along with spiritual principles for one is the how things work and the what things are respectively. So let's start at the top. We love you Abundance, we love the surplus of resources for us to easily give our tithes and offerings and the means to pay ourselves before any other bills are paid. It should be at least 10% of our gross income. This must be a priority because we must honor your ability and have confidence that if we create margin to build wealth, you will expand also to make a way. Thank you. Thank you for the great experiences of travel and beautiful memories we are able to collect enjoying Five Star resorts, going to exotic and historical locations around the world. Thank you for cancelling all debt in less than ten years, including our mortgage, so we are no longer slaves to the lender. Thank you for ample amounts for setting up our children and their children's

> It may not go exactly as planned but stay the course.

> There will be setbacks, mistakes and mishaps along the way, but don't waver.

> There will be adjustments needed and alternate strategies used but stay true to your core values.

> There may be adversaries who appear or new alliances that may be formed throughout, but be wise.

> The cost of time, energy, and resources may seem unreasonable, but pay the price.

Be Willing To Make All Sacrifices

Pay the price of admission to your next level of success. What you have known and what you have done has got you to your present level of financial success or failure. If you do nothing different and simply try to dismiss the process, your results will likely be the same. In other words, you cannot remain the same person you are and go to where you must go. You must change your thinking, so you may change your habits, so you may change your life.

GET RE-CONDITIONED TO ACT LIKE A WINNER

There are **Five Routine Practices** suggested among personal and professional development coaches and organizations for their clients or patrons which are:

1) Read at least one book a month or one article a day via finance, business or personal development.

Note: Reading is a must for stimulating ideas and strategies around finance and business. The more you know and apply, the more you will grow as a person.

2) Listen to one to three audios a day. It can be audio books, it can

financial future. Thank you for providing a stress free and debt free retirement. We appreciate that the more we focus on contributing back to the world, bringing greater value, the more resources you give us to work with and be grateful for.

We take responsibility for our relationship not being fruitful because we are the cause of our external effect based on how we talk, think, and feel. Our thoughts become things, be it both positive or negative and if we vibrate at a higher frequency, the like frequency that carry the equivalent of human resources, intellectual resources, financial resources, etc. become available to bring the ideas to past. We now realize, like a genie in a bottle, you can be whatever we desire you to be. You can be a master, a hard taskmaster who demands we chase you, serve you and do whatever, go wherever, and spend whatever time necessary to please you...or treat you as the servant where whatever we desire to have, go, and do, you will present ample funds or grace (favor) for us to accomplish or reach our goals. You stand ready to go to work on our behalf and we are sorry we did not have more confidence in you or understand your true purpose to serve.

So Abundance, despite the scarcity mind conditioning we have been accustomed to, we will budget and save and give definite purpose and aim to you being more productive. From now on, we will make sure you are excited about being in this relationship, being busy helping us have a means to doing, having, and being a greater blessing to our family, community, and church. We will not hoard money but will be a conduit where you continually flow through our lives for the benefit of others. We will talk often and be committed to our vow of loving you till death do us part and showing our appreciation. We will learn all of the ways to be wise stewards of what you have given us and grant you your authority to meet and exceed the expectations in our life. We look forward to a wonderful life together.

— $ TAKE BACK YOUR WEALTH! $ —

be inspirational YouTube clips on the Anthony Robbins, Zig Ziglar's, Les Browns and Eric Thompsons of the world.

Note: You must push out the negative criticism of yourself. You have been conditioned to see yourself as small, as helpless and insignificant. You must be re-conditioned to see yourself as the giant and the superhero you were meant to be.

3) Be in association with like-minded people at least once a week and as often as you can. We are better together. This includes trainings, life groups, seminars, workshops, networking events, social communities and so on.

Note: There are at least two ways to learn a new language. Buy Rosetta Stone or be immersed in the culture. Being immersed in the culture helps you to learn and apply faster, be inspired, be supported, and be held accountable by those who are moving in the same direction as you are.

4) Watch your diet and exercise. "Your first wealth is your health." Balance is the key.

Note: Your energy level, your mental and physical stamina, your longevity is dependent on your good health. Change takes time and you must endure the process.

5) Apply what you are learning daily. Practice until it is made perfect and if you don't reach perfection, at least you will be excellent.

Note: "Without a struggle, there is no progress." Make the tough decisions and make the necessary steps toward greater.

Moving from Lack to *Abundance*

THE ART OF WAR AND MONEY

Tani is hanging out with her adult sons over the weekend and they all went to see the movie titled *Art of War*.

Tani: I love our mommy and son dates. You will always be my babies. Thanks for seeing this movie with me. Being an army veteran, I am attracted to war-type movies.

Son #1: I know mom, we don't mind. You get so excited watching movies like *Lone Survivor* or *Unbroken*.

Tani: Okay guys, time for your life lessons. There are five things to know in the art of war being very similar to the art of chess, what are they?

Son #2: Oh boy, here we go. I forgot that, what intrigues you the most is the strategies used in combat.

Son #1: Yes…I think I know because I figured there would be a lesson afterwards.

One—Be willing to make all sacrifices.

Two—Know your opponent and yourself.

Three—Know the rules of engagement.

Four—Be patient with your own plan; I forgot the last one.

Tani: That was good, the last rule the Captain mentioned was to capitalize on time. How can each rule be used in your own finances?

Son #2: Mom, why must you always relate these lessons to money?

Tani: It is because I was not taught money principles growing up, and I only did fairly well due to my military retirement and social security benefits, but I want

—$ **TAKE BACK YOUR WEALTH!** $—

Questions For Review & Reflection:

1) Who are you vs. a consumer, borrower, and laborer?

_____

2) What is the Three in One System? What is each entity specialty?

_____

3) What does D.I.R.T stand for?

_____

4) How can you capitalize on time in your lifetime to accomplish more financially?

_____

5) What is one routine practice you can do to shift your thinking and your actions?

_____

Moving from **Lack** to *Abundance*

you to do a lot better than I did, so you must know the rules and how to execute.

Son #1: I'm game. Be patient with own plan. So that means I should save and invest for the long term and not be distracted by the economy or life situations that come up along the way. If I want to buy something, be patient to save up to buy it free and clear. If I start a business, realize it will take a minimum of three to five years to turn a profit and be duplicatable, so I must be patient in finance and business.

Tani: Very good, what's next?

Son #2: Know your opponent and yourself. There is D.I.R.T that is made up of four forces that seek to come against my finances.

Tani: Yes, that's good. It looks like you are retaining some knowledge.

Son #2: Yes Mom, since you joined the Family Wealth Community, you've been making sure we are financially savvy. So D stands for debt which tries to entrap me for my life. There is I for Inflation which can diminish my purchasing power. R is for Retirement vehicles which can be ineffective with high fees, volatile growth, and taxable consequences and T is for Taxes which can keep me working into my elder years if I don't learn how to minimize my tax liability throughout my life, so I may redirect my monies toward building wealth. Knowing myself, is reminding myself that I am an owner and wealth builder. A wise man said, *"If I don't know who I am and where I am going, someone will tell me who I am and where I am going, and it will typically be less than what I deserve."* How was that mom

CHAPTER # TWO

PRELUDE TO FIVE STAR SUCCESS

— Moving from **Lack** to *Abundance* —

FAMILY WEALTH COMMUNITY
ENGAGEMENT OF CONCEPTS
-Continued-

—$ **TAKE BACK YOUR WEALTH!** $—

THERE ARE TIMELESS PRACTICES

There are **Five Money Rules** that are key to financial success. If learned as early as three years old and followed throughout life, it will serve a person well to enjoy financial success. At any age, it is not too late to learn and apply. The **Five Money Rules** are:

1) PAY YOURSELF FIRST. Preserve 10% Minimum.

2) GIVE 10% TO A WORTHY CAUSE.

3) SAVE FOR EMERGENCY FUND & FUTURE PURCHASES.

4) MINIMIZE TAXES & DEBT And Reallocate.

5) MANAGE SPENDING With A Plan.

PAY YOURSELF FIRST

Before paying the cable bill, the electric bill, the gas bill...Before paying the car note or the cell phone bill...Before getting the nails and hair done, PAY YOURSELF FIRST! Without you, nothing works and since you are responsible for your today and tomorrow, a portion of all you earn should be put aside for such purposes. The younger you must take care of the older you. Since Social Security is becoming bankrupt, pensions are almost obsolete, and average savings are dismal, there must a priority on preserving a portion of your income, 10% or more for lifetime (i.e. lifetime income) and for legacy purposes (surplus that remain beyond your lifetime).

This rule is not new. The concept was expressed in the Richest Man In Babylon where the citizens of Babylon were being taught how to build riches and wealth 5000 years ago.

Moving from **Lack to** *Abundance*

Tani: That was excellent! I like that quote. What else?

Son #1: Batter up! Be willing to make all sacrifices. It sounds like, be willing to take losses but that should not apply when investing or saving money. I don't have to accept high risk in order to receive decent returns. Mom, you say never lose your principal, so it does not mean be willing to take a loss. However, it just occurred to me, that shaving down some of my expenses, i.e. cable, cell phone, or eating out can be worthwhile sacrifices to redirect toward building my lifetime and legacy wealth.

Tani: You two are making me proud. What's next?

Son #1: I think I am on a roll. Another one is capitalize on time. Being I have two babies, you started a Wealth Legacy Plan on one and you suggested that you wanted me to get a Wealth Legacy Plan for the second child, to start building cash savings and wealth throughout their lifetime and beyond. I also realize that since I am turning 29 years old, I have time to grow my wealth and enjoy tax free retirement with no risk or loss of principal with my own Wealth Legacy Plan regardless of the market volatility. I like that!

Son #2: Okay, let's see. We talked about 1) Be patient with own plan, 2) Know your opponent, 3) Be willing to make all sacrifices, 4) Capitalize on time and the last one is 5) Know the rules of engagement. I think this one is the most important of all because we all must know the rules of money. Like in the movie, we saw the various branches of military service have their battle plans, their enemy capture protocol, being caught behind enemy lines, guerilla tactics and so on. They had to be prepared for going on the offense, defense, retreat, and on to victory. My money is the same way. I must know my offensive position, my defensive position, and how to win the game. Without knowing how money works and how to capitalize on its use, unfortunately I can be defeated over and over again. I can be held hostage for my time, labor, and resources. That won't

TAKE BACK YOUR WEALTH!

"A part of all you earn is yours to keep. It should not be less than a tenth no matter how little you earn." - Richest Man In Babylon

Wealth takes time and money sown early enough can compound (double, triple, quadruple, etc.) into a harvest. The discipline of putting money away for long-term growth purposes without touching them is what is taught in the affluent families around the world.

GIVE 10% TO A WORTHY CAUSE

Giving 10% is a spiritual principle. The gesture signifies being thankful for needs being met and giving back to the universe for others needs to be met also. The 10% represents the belief in abundance, the overflow from one person or entity to another.

In giving, it does not have to be just money, there can be time and talents shared with the universe as well. There is a bountiful measure given back in one form or another. This concept is the Universal Law (and Principle) of Reciprocity.

SAVE FOR EMERGENCY FUND & FUTURE PURCHASES

Many financial planners recommend saving a minimum of $1,000 to start, up to three to six months of expenses for emergency purposes, i.e. car repairs, appliance repairs, doctors visit, traveling to visit a sick loved one, etc. Emergencies are inevitable. They will appear in one form or another at an inconvenient time, so the best you can do is prepare for when it happens. "Life Happens" can be a t-shirt.

Future purchases are items and experiences desired sometime in the near future, perhaps six months out, one year out, two years out, etc. Saving up for future purchases is called delayed gratification meaning, there is first a sacrifice of time and a discipline of money saved to receive the reward of the desired item or experience. This is in direct opposition to the philosophy of immediate gratification and the practice or use of credit card purchases. You are sold via Mastercard and Visa commercials that you have to have it right now with no delay.

Moving from Lack to *Abundance*

happen to me...I can promise you that.

Tani: I am glad to hear you say that. So, what will you do to ensure you will win financially?

Son #2: I am going to pay attention and heed your advice. I am not going to fall asleep during my 20s and 30s and wake up at age 40 or 50 being frantic about becoming a statistic. I am 24 years old and I am making some solid moves with my money now. I set up my Wealth Legacy Plan about two months ago and I am participating in the 401(k) Plan because the company is matching dollar for dollar on the job. I have about 15% total being put away from paying myself first, 6% on the job and the other 9% going into my Wealth Legacy Plan; plus, another 10%, I am saving for emergencies and future purchases.

Tani: That is great son, that is why I love having these conversations and lessons with you all because I want you to be sensitive to the world around you and how to maneuver properly in it. I am going to have to depend on you two to educate your brother and sister also. Thank you for obliging your mother for our mom and son dates.

THE RULES ABOUT MONEY

Over the course of the week, usually on Sundays, Shaughn Lee, Aviance, and the twins gather for their family meetings or finance lessons.

Shaughn Lee: Okay, settle down boys, let's get started with our financial lesson today. Sweetie are you ready?

Aviance: Yes, I am coming. Does anyone want anything while I am in the kitchen? Going once, going twice.

—$ TAKE BACK YOUR WEALTH! $—

Remember the Three in One System. The more debt you have, the more interest you pay, the less wealth you create for you, your family and your legacy. You have two choices, continue to feed the system or begin to build your wealth. Which is more important?

MINIMIZE TAXES

When it comes to taxes, there are numerous ways to reduce taxes legally. The purpose of reducing tax liability is to have more active and passive income preserved for building own wealth. You also want to reduce tax liability when transferring assets from one generation to another.

You have to be knowledgeable and strategic about reducing taxes all throughout the year, not just during tax time. Tax breaks favor the business owner, the landowner, and the investor, in other words tax breaks cater to the owner and wealth builder.

To be strategic, consider these various methods for reducing tax liability.

1) An employee can increase tax withholding allowances on W-4 to pay less taxes and have more take home pay. In the words of a Tax Practitioner, *"STOP EXPECTING LARGE RETURNS DURING TAX SEASON!"* Why pay $8K in taxes to get $4K back? Why not break even with the government where you don't owe them and they don't owe you. Speak to your tax advisor about this technique.

Note: Based on historical Tax Freedom Day Chart in 2017, the chart showed how employees worked 21 days in 1900 and how they worked 114 (almost 1/3 of 365 days) to pay taxes in 2016. Therefore, employees are working more days to pay taxes to the government before reaping the benefits of own labor.

2) Employee vs. Corporation tax priority is quite the opposite. As an employee, there is a tax withholding from an employee's paycheck, meaning taxes are paid before the employee gets paid then the employee attempts to pay living expenses, manage debt, and try to save and invest with very little to work with.

As an owner of a corporation, the business can acquire assets (i.e.

 Moving from Lack to *Abundance*

Twin #1: Yes mom, I will have some raisin snacks please.

Twin #2: Can I have some apple juice please? Thanks mom.

Shaughn Lee: I'm good. Thanks anyway...Okay family, today we are going to learn about the Five Rules of Money. How many of you want to have a financially successful life (Everyone raises their hands)? Great, so you want to win financially and live the life you imagine for yourself, right? (Everyone nods and gestures in agreement). So, let me ask you this: If you had a puzzle and you had to assemble the pieces in the box to form the picture on top of the box, could you do it if all of the pieces of the puzzle were not in the box?

Twin #2: No dad. I wouldn't be able to complete the picture. (The others nod in agreement).

Shaughn Lee: Well, you are absolutely correct and that is what happens to the majority of Americans who do not know the rules of money. It is like not having all of the pieces of a puzzle and yet seeking to live a completed picture life. However, most never complete the picture or live the life they imagined. Today, we are going to discuss best practices based on Five Money Rules... Where's your notebook or iPad? Take notes. I'm learning a lot at our Family Wealth Empowerment meetings, so I am eager to share.

✋ The Five Money Rules are:

1) Pay Yourself First, Preserve 10% Minimum.

2) Give 10% To A Worthy Cause.

3) Save For Emergency Fund And Future Purchases.

4) Minimize Taxes & Debt, Then Reallocate.

5) Manage Spending With A Plan.

Let's go through each. Tell me what do you think they mean.

equipment, real estate, vehicles, etc.), then pay expenses related to acquisition and business operations, write off debt payments, and pay taxes last. The business (corporation) owner can build wealth much faster than the employee simply because there are more resources to work with at the beginning vs. the end. See illustration below.

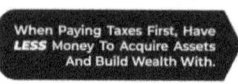 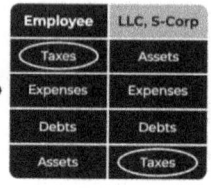

3) Another method for reducing the tax liability is being aware of **Five Tax Advantage Strategies** and they are as follows.

A. Credits are a dollar reduction in the tax bill. If in 28% tax bracket, then a deduction of $100 saves $28.00 in tax, but a credit of $100 saves $100 on tax bill. Examples are Earned Income Tax Credit, Child & Dependent Care Credit, Research Tax Credit, etc.

B. Exclusions are benefits that are not counted as income such as Workers Compensation, Borrowed Money, Scholarships, Hospitalization Premiums Paid By Employer, etc.

C. Deductions are often used due to business expenses, debt, and acquisitions. There are above the line and below the line deductions.

D. Tax Shelters are for foregoing or deferring tax liability such as 401(k)s, IRAs, Cash Value Insurance, Trust, Annuities, Foundations, etc.

E. Investments which are short term capital gains, are investments sold within the first year. Gains are taxed at ordinary income tax rate. Long-

Moving from Lack to *Abundance*

Aviance: I'll go. Pay yourself first means before I pay for lights, gas, or get my hair and nails done, I am going to set aside 10% minimum of my gross pay for long term wealth. "General" says, the young man or woman must take care of the older man or woman. It is no one else's responsibility but my own, so I pay myself because it is my responsibility to myself.

Shaughn Lee: It's important. No doubt. It is easier said than done. How do you manage to put the 10% or more aside, sweetie?

Aviance: I have always had three personal accounts and I still have them beyond our joint accounts. One is a checking account for paying bills, i.e. car note, personal credit cards, my braces, my pampering me massages, etc. The second account is a saving account for wealth building. That is where the 10% or more goes. I have a set amount direct deposited into my account per pay period. Out of sight, out of mind.

Twin #2: What about the 401(k) on your job, mom? Are you putting money into your retirement plan on the job too?

Aviance: Look at my baby boy. What do you know about 401(k)s? You are too smart. Well darling, I am still putting money into it. However, not as much since I found out about all of the fees, stipulations, penalties, and tax consequences. Furthermore, if I was not vested (usually around three to five year period) with the company, I would switch vehicles altogether for less risk, more consistent returns, more sickness and death benefits, and more predictable lifetime tax-free income benefits. This is why I shifted money over and above the company match to what we call the Wealth Legacy Plan which is my own financial system.

Twin #2: That's different, mom, I haven't heard about putting money into a Wealth Legacy Plan vs. 401(k)?

term capital gains are investments sold, over one year or more. Gains are taxed at capital gains rate (i.e. 0 to 20% in 2018).

When choosing investment vehicles, it is important to classify them into three categories: Taxable, Tax Deferred, and Tax-Free. Your financial vehicle chosen, and tax strategy determines the amount of wealth grown and available for distribution.

TAXABLE	TAX DEFERRED	TAX FREE
Checking Saving CD Money Market Mutual Funds Index Funds	401(k) 457 IRA 403(b) Annuity	Cash Value Insurance Roth IRA Roth 401(k)
Taxable On Gains	Taxable on Distribution	Tax Free Distribution

For example, imagine $1 being doubled each day for twenty days, and the tax bracket is 25%. If the gains are **taxable** in first column after each gain, the $1 doubled for twenty days accumulates to $72,570. If the $1 is doubled for twenty days **tax deferred,** then the 25% comes off when distributed, accumulating $783,472 and if $1 doubled for twenty days **tax-free**, the result is $1,048,576.

— Moving from Lack to *Abundance* —

Aviance: I know. I didn't know anything about it either until I saw both financial tools and strategies compared side by side. I was blown away by what I didn't know, and the benefits of the Wealth Legacy Plan clearly outweighed the 401(k) in my opinion, so it was an easy decision to make. For example, what makes more sense to pay taxes on the smaller amount of the money like the seed or pay taxes on the larger amount of the money like the harvest?

Twin #1: I'd pay taxes on the smaller amount. (Twin #2 agrees).

Aviance: Exactly! If I was not already vested, I would care less about reducing my gross income by putting money into it and instead, in my youth I would have taken advantage of a more effective savings/investment account with money accessible after a short time period with no restrictions, penalties, or permission required before age 59.5. I would have capitalized on the tax advantages of the growth, withdrawal or loan, distribution in my elder years and transfer of wealth for my babies and generational heirs. (The boys give a blank stare at each other. Shaughn Lee smiles hearing how passionate Aviance has become even though speaking over the boy's heads at this time) It's never too late, this is why I have money over and above the company match from my job transferred to my savings account then a certain amount transferred to the Wealth Legacy Plan.

Twin #2: (Trying his best to connect) It seems like everyone should be able to choose between several different kinds of products for their best benefit.

Aviance: You are right darling. Let me continue. The second savings account is for saving for emergencies and future purchases. Because things always happen at one point in time, like me having to hop a flight immediately to see my sister who was in a car accident, or fixing the washing machine when it broke last month. For future purchases, money is saved up for trips like our family Disney Vacation or Mardi Gras trip in Louisiana or for the five-day Caribbean cruise your father and I are planning this summer. etc. I usually put 10% of my gross income into the second savings account as well. The financial planner typically

An example of all three columns are below:

DAYS	TAXABLE	TAX DEFERRED	TAX FREE
Day 1	$1 x 2 less. 25% = $1.75	$1 x 2 = $2	$1 x 2 = $2
Day 20	Day 19 x 2 less 25% = 72,570.64	Day 19 x 2 = 1,048,576.00	Day 19 x 2 = 1,048,576.00
RESULT	$72,570.64	Less 25% = $786,472	$1,048,576.00

Which category is best for having the most income or lump sums at the end of a period of time?

Finally, there are tax considerations when real assets are transferred to a spouse or heirs. There are death taxes which consist of inheritance taxes and estate taxes. All of the nuances of estate tax laws are above the scope of this book. Refer to an Estate Planning Strategist to learn how to pay little to no taxes upon receipt of an inheritance.

Setting up a Trust before death helps to pass assets to heirs without having to deal with state probate requirements and associated expenses. You can also move assets around when having a Durable or General Power of Attorney before death of loved one and transfer car or recreation vehicle titles or home deeds over from loved one to self or heirs. Setting up a POD (Paid on death) designation on checking or saving accounts or having beneficiaries on life insurance policies, investment accounts, etc. can set up immediate transfer of assets without probate as well.

MINIMIZE DEBT

It cannot be expressed enough how debt, which is principal plus margin (interest) must be ideally eliminated on the personal side of your financial affairs.

The average American carries about 35% in total debt vs. their gross

suggests three to six months in savings for emergency purposes.

Twin #1: Wow, you really got it together, mom. That's how I am going to be.

Shaughn Lee: Son, I am grateful for your mom because we are on the same page when it comes to money and we hold each other accountable with our disciplines to reach our financial goals.

Twin #2: We're grateful for both of our parents. Keep up the great work!

Shaughn Lee: Thanks, son, for your approval rating. It's appreciated. Let's move to the next rule which is give 10% to a worthy cause. Who can explain what that means to you?

Twin #1: I think I can explain. Giving is a spiritual principle, that's what we talked about in our youth group at church. Giving with a cheerful heart and being generous with time, talent, and treasure brings more in return. So, our giving can be giving of our time at the soup kitchen or helping out at Samaritans Feet or giving funds to a church or a charitable institution like the McDonald's house or cure for muscular dystrophy, etc... What about lending my talented, beautiful singing voice to a play or school choir? Is that being generous?

Twin #2: I am sure your school wishes you kept that voice to yourself and wasn't so generous (the family chuckles). However, I hear what you are saying bro. I have found when helping others, I have less to complain about and more to be thankful for. I understand that money rule loud and clear.

Shaughn Lee: This is awesome! Because our financial lessons aren't about reciting information, it is very much about making the information relevant to each of our lives. Your mom did a great job explaining the saving for emergency fund and future purchases, so let's move on to minimize taxes and debt, then reallocate. Why is this important? I'll answer this one myself. Taxes and debt are

income. That is $35 of debt payments out of $100 of income made. If paying too much debt, there is no room for paying yourself first, giving and saving? Let's examine closer.

If there is $5,000 in gross income for a person and 25% is the federal and state tax combined rates and 35% is the average debt serviced per month, then the following scenario follows:

Traditional Habits

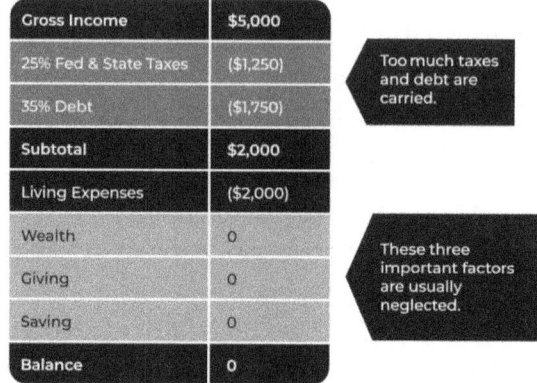

Due to paying so much in taxes and debt, there is very little, if anything, left for long-term saving/investing, giving, emergency fund, or future purchases. The order must be shifted beforehand to minimize, re-prioritize, and reallocate.

Better Habits

When reducing taxes to 15% and debt to 10% in illustration below, money can be re-prioritized and reallocated to building wealth, being more generous in giving, and preparing for life's emergencies or saving up for future purchases vs. financing via credit cards or loans. Immediately, your money flow is reversed from the government and banks to you, your family, your future, and your legacy.

Moving from **Lack** to *Abundance*

two of four forces that come against our money. We pay all kinds of taxes such as sales tax, property tax, sin taxes for cigarettes and beer, payroll taxes from our pay, federal and state taxes, etc. And we don't have to pay more than our share. There was an article which talked about how Warren Buffett (a billionaire) with primary stock holdings in Berkshire Hathaway paid 17% in overall taxes while his secretary reported paying 33%. Warren Buffett gives a perfect example of how to get tax breaks.

Twin #1: Whoa Dad, you mean a billionaire paid almost half in taxes compared to his secretary? Those are some definite tax breaks.

Shaughn Lee: That's right, son. Tax breaks go to the corporation owner, the investor, and land owner. Business owners actually pay taxes last after acquiring things of value, like property or business equipment, paying the expenses related to being in business and business debt. Being an employee, a laborer for a company or the government, unfortunately pays taxes first, then expenses, debt, and they have a lot less to acquire assets (things that make money or have lasting value) like gold, silver, commercial real estate, stocks and bonds, etc. For debt, it has been a lingering statistic stating how the average American has 35% of every $1 or $35 out of $100 made being paid to service debt. The problem with debt, is the longer it takes to pay off an item, or experience, the more wealth is created for whom?

Twin #2: The longer it takes to pay off anything with interest attached, the more we make the banks rich and wealthy. The faster we pay off the debt, the more wealth we can build for ourselves.

Shaughn Lee: I am so proud of my family! We should be awarded Family of the Year on somebody's stage… Eliminating debt is easy with discipline. We are taught as a Family Wealth community to pay off all debt on our personal side

— $ **TAKE BACK YOUR WEALTH!** $ —

Gross Income	$5,000
Wealth @ 10%	($500)
Giving @ 10%	($500)
Savings @ 10%	($500)
Subtotal	**$3,500**
Living Expenses	($2,000)
Taxes @ 15%	($1000)
Debt @ 105	($500)
Balance	**0**

Yes! — When re-prioritizing, more can be accomplished.

Reduce tax liability and carry lower to no debt.

MANAGE EXPENSES WITH A PLAN

Live within your means and expand your means! The basic discipline of budgeting denotes how much is coming in from all income sources and how much is going out in expenses and debt. Remember,

"Budgeting is for today and saving is for tomorrow. Both are equally important." - Rodney Archer

A financial worksheet is a great exercise for individuals and couples as well as business owners. The Family Wealth Financial Worksheet is made up of Part I: Expense Statement, Part II: a Balance Sheet to determine, Part III: Discretionary Income (amount left over after expenses and debt payments) and Net Worth (assets minus liabilities, minus taxes if liquidating).

Go to **worksheet.familywealthtoday.com** to fill out Excel Spreadsheet, then schedule to talk to a Wealth Strategist. The worksheet should be filled out at least once a year for personal or business finance purposes. The income and expenses are important to manage. This is called Cash Flow Management, maximizing inflow and minimizing outflow.

of the ledger and live debt free in the fastest time possible. When mastering the basics, then we learn how to leverage credit for perks and a greater return. The business side of the ledger is where leverage, borrowing, and building assets takes place mostly, imitating the banks strategies. I won't go into the details of that strategy right now.

Twin #1: You said that billionaire guy owns stocks, how does that help lower his taxes, Dad?

Shaughn Lee: Ok, you picked up on that. That's a little off subject but I will say there are capital gains from buying stocks at a low price and selling at a higher price and there are dividends which are company profits being shared with shareholders. Both can have a 15% tax bracket vs. regular income bracket of 25% or higher.

Twin #2: That's how that guy paid so much less than his working-class secretary, right?

Shaughn Lee: Yes.

Twin #1: Dad, I never heard any of our friends talk about learning this stuff at home. You have us in a charter school among some pretty rich people, whose parents are judges, engineers, bankers, accountants, etc. Are you part of a secret society or something?

Shaughn Lee: (Aviance and Shaughn Lee look at each other and grin). No son, your mother and I have been telling you that we have been learning all of this from our Family Wealth community. Listen to this truth, *"An academic education is for earning a living, a financial education is for building lifetime and legacy wealth."* Both types of education are needed.

Twin #1: All I know bro, if our parents are this sharp on their finances and

—$ TAKE BACK YOUR WEALTH! $—

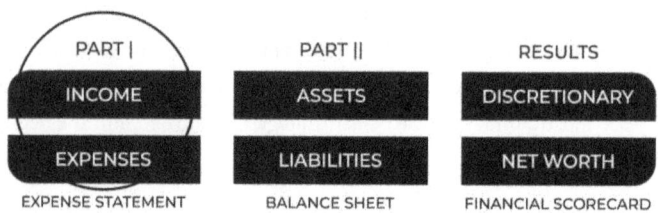

A monthly budgeting form or web application has Income and Expense items (including Debt Items) listed with Projections and Actuals. Discretionary Income is determined when Expense/Debt Items are subtracted from Net Income. This form can be an Excel or Google Spreadsheet.

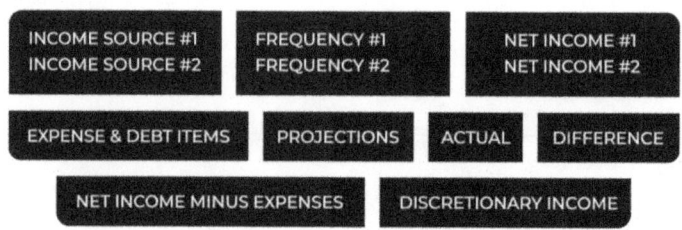

Go to **budget.familywealthtoday.com** for Excel form to fill out. Mint.com created by Intuit and producer of QuickBooks, is a FREE online budgeting tool equally good for personal and business finance.

Beware of the following when minimizing outflow:

    1) ATM charges. You can be charged $3 at foreign ATMs and $3 at your banking institution.

Note: This is wasteful! Plan your purchases for the day, use your debit card or go to your bank's ATM.

— Moving from **Lack** to *Abundance* —

we are the heirs of this information and the estate, we are going to be pretty financially savvy ourselves.

Twin #2: No doubt. I am already feeling like I am going to be a financial giant in my lifetime. What about reallocating once taxes and debt are minimized or eliminated though?

Aviance: I'll answer that. Once taxes and debt are minimized, then money used to pay taxes and service debt are reallocated or redistributed towards building more wealth, giving more, saving more, or enjoying life more with traveling, dining, etc.

Shaughn Lee: Wow! I can see everyone is really into what we are talking about. Let me back up a minute. I did not tell you how anyone can pay down the debt as fast as possible.

Twin #2: Oh yeah, how do you do that?

Shaughn Lee: Okay, if you have four debts already, let's say there are two credit cards, a car note, and student loan. Hypothetically speaking...because you two boys won't experience this scenario for a few years yet, let me draw it out...

Item	Balance	Payment
Credit Card #1	$2,000	$35
Credit Card #2	$1,500	$25
Car Note	$12,000	$350
Student Loan	$18,000	$250

—$ TAKE BACK YOUR *W*EALTH! $—

2) Bank Fees. There are overdraft fees, monthly checking or saving account fees, over the limit fees, and/or annual fees for credit cards.

Note: Set up overdraft protection saving accounts to link to checking accounts. When using debit card, balance transactions daily. Ask how to avoid monthly checking and saving account fees altogether. Keep credit card balances low as well as paid off monthly. Step up to low to no annual fee credit cards after establishing credit.

3) High cable, internet, or cell phone bills. Make sure unwanted extras have not been added or remain after promotional period.

Note: Review once a year. Buy phone and notebooks outright and get better rates with no contract, month to month billing.

4) Excessive Dining Out Expenses.

Note: Set daily spending limits, i.e. $10, $15, or $20 a day. Cook as much as possible to eat more healthy, reducing the dining cost.

5) Excessive Travel or Extracurricular Activities. All things should be done in moderation.

Note: Remember discretionary income is not just for fun and leisure, it should be for wealth building, giving, and saving first. Reducing taxes and debt can be reallocated for fun and leisure.

6) Increasing Home, Auto, and Health Insurance.

Note: Shop around once a year to ensure you are getting the best rates. You can also accept higher deductibles for lower monthly premiums.

7) High Rent Districts or Upscale Neighborhoods. Everything will cost you a little more in areas such as the dry cleaners, grocery stores, homeowner association dues, rent, etc.

Note: Living a little further from the hotspots can give you twice the space for half the price. Make sure you don't live among the upper class too soon, if you don't have upper class money and wealth building habits.

8) Cash Advance and Check Cashing Places. You will pay a premium for the short-term loan or for cashing each check.

Note: Pay your previous outstanding banking balances and get your regular banking relationship re-established to avoid fees on check cashing.

Moving from **Lack** to *Abundance*

Okay, now you see the balances of the various items and the payments required. There is debt elimination software to include interest rates and mortgages. We are taught to eliminate ALL debt in ten years or less. In this example, if you did nothing different and did not add any more debt onto the credit cards or simply paid at the banks pay back schedule, guess how long it would take to pay back or pay off all debt?

Twin #2: About five years?

Twin #1: About seven years?

Shaughn Lee: Good try. What about twenty-five years?

Twin #1: No way! Who pays on debt for twenty-five years? That sounds crazy mad.

Aviance: Unfortunately, a lot of people, son.

Shaughn Lee: So, I think we can agree it is not a good idea to just pay at the banks schedule. Right? (Family nods in agreement). A proven way to pay down all debt faster is to have a debt accelerator which is using discretionary income of let's say $200 per month from minimizing taxes and debt. When $200 is added to credit card #2 with a $25 payment, it is paid off in less than seven months. Then $225 is added to $35 payment to pay off credit card #1's $2000 balance in another seven months. When $260 is added to the $350 payment to pay off car notes $12k balance, it is paid off in another 14 months. And when adding $610 per month to $250 per month payment for student loan remaining $18k balance, it is paid off in another 14 months, so $33,500 in total debt is paid off in approximately 42 months or 3.5 years. WOW!!

Aviance: Also, in that example $800 per month is freed up to reallocate towards wealth building, giving, saving, or more leisure. Is that right, boo?

Shaughn Lee: Y'all see why I call her my sweetie (the boys look at each other

9) Rent To Own Furniture or Buy Here, Pay Here Car Lots. Without excellent credit or saved up cash for future purchases, you can have less quality for a higher priced item, paying for a longer period of time.

Note: Save up to buy quality furniture and reliable cars. Finance when necessary to pay off quickly.

10) Title Loans and High Interest Loans.

Note: High interest loans can be 10% or higher with short time frames of one year or less for pay back. Thirty percent or higher are 'gangster rates.' Beware!

Remember that your money has purpose, it has to take care of your today needs and your tomorrow wealth, so all money has to be accounted for to maximize efficiency and ensure the most progress throughout your lifetime.

THERE ARE BUSINESS BEST PRACTICES

If you are going to increase your income streams passively, you have two choices, one is to buy into or build a business system or two is let money make money in an investment.

Let's focus on the business system which can be used in order to create passive and recurring income. You can always hunt or chase down the next customer or take excellent care of the customer that you have, that he or she will be excited to let others know about you. Let's create the right atmosphere.

"Chase excellence and money will chase you!" - Dr. George Fraser

Make sure you are in business for the right reasons. If you aren't genuinely interested in what you are offering to the marketplace, your success will be limited. Everyone can see a hustler coming with sales breath, i.e. an image of a man with an overcoat in the summer heat with jewelry on one side and toiletries on the other.

— Moving from **Lack** to *Abundance* —

and giggle). We are almost done. The last money rule is manage your expenses, live with a plan. In order to manage expenses, there must be a budget or spending limit daily, weekly, and monthly.

Aviance: I have a daily spending budget for eating out which is about $10 a day. That forces me to fix my lunch or take leftovers for my lunch at work. I may not eat out a few days and then splurge on a nice $25 meal one day. Spending limits are just parameters we put on ourselves, so we may accomplish more in other areas of our financial lives.

Shaughn Lee: That's right, we must know how much money is coming in and monitor how much is going out each month for greater control. This discipline ensures money is used for other important matters. As a recap of our lesson, before paying expenses, pay yourself a minimum of 10 percent, give 10 percent to a worthy cause, save roughly 10 percent for emergency fund and future purchases, reduce taxes and debt so there is more for investments or for creating precious memories.

Twin #1: Dad, that was a lot of information, but it seems like once bro man and I fully grasp the concepts, we would be unstoppable. What do you think?

Shaughn Lee: You two will be great and that is what your mother and I are counting on.

A week goes by and a special guest business affiliate is asked to help speak on the topic of building businesses effectively and to scale.

Pastor Sean: I hope everyone has had a great week? (Everyone nods in agreement). We will go around the room to get your latest activity next week. Today, we have Demond who is the CEO of StealthEnomics as a special guest and strategic partner for our infrastructure technology support behind many of our community projects. Amen. I will defer the floor to "General" who will conduct an interview with Demond for our topic today.

—$ TAKE BACK YOUR *WEALTH!* $—

Remember, business is about building relationships and if you are not building relationships, you have no business being in business.

✋ Follow the **Five P's For Developing Core Business Model** and they are:

PURPOSE—Your business should line up with your reason for living. This will also give you passion about what you are presenting to the marketplace.

PEOPLE—The motivation should be to make life better for mankind, to leave people in better shape than when you found them. Also, seek to find a team of people who can support your vision.

PRODUCTS—What product or service can serve people best, that is better, cheaper, or faster than what exists?

PROCESSES—What infrastructure, operations, and marketing methods can attract or what manufacturing and distribution models can deliver on demand?

PROFITS—What is the margin over cost? Does it compare in price with competitors? What is the breakeven amount that must be sold before yielding a profit? What is the net profit after cost of goods and operational expenses?

✋ To become a **Five Star Company**, a client must answer Yes to all five of these questions and they are:

1) Is there great value as far as there being great quality for the price?

2) Does the representative have a professional appearance and are they knowledgeable about the product or service?

3) Is there timely delivery and follow through with what is being offered or sold?

4) Is there good customer service: being attentive, courteous, and friendly at all times?

5) Is experience so outstanding that others should be told about the business or products and services offered?

— Moving from **Lack** to *Abundance* —

QUALITY SERVICE, DELIVERY, & FOLLOWING

"GENERAL:" Thank you Pastor Sean. Hello everyone, it is a pleasure to see you all again. Today, we are going to discuss Five Star Service as it pertains to building business systems. This is why I asked Demond to be here tonight as he and his team at StealthEnomics, exemplify what this means. Five Star Service is about getting a client and keeping a client and getting them to be a referrer for you and your business. Five questions are asked:

1) Is there great value? Is there great quality for the price?

2) Does the representatives have a professional appearance and are they knowledgeable about products or services offered?

3) Is there timely delivery and follow through with what is being offered?

4) Is there good customer service? Is the representative courteous and friendly at all times?

5) Is the client inclined to tell others about the business, products, or service?

Come on up Demond and share your philosophy around being a Five Star Service Company.

Demond: Thanks "General." What does it take to be a Five Star Success Company? Consider the Five P's.

#1 You as the business owner must have <u>purpose</u> and passion for what you do.

#2 Seek to serve <u>people</u>, to meet a need in the marketplace.

#3 Determine what <u>product</u> will best meet the need.

#4 What <u>processes</u> are in place to distribute the product in massive quantities?

#5 What are the <u>profit</u> margins to be competitive and offer great value?

SYSTEMS OF DOMINATION

There are **Five Money Systems** devised by the Elite of our society worldwide: Credit, Cash Flow, Business, Banking, and Investments. These five money systems move money and make money, oftentimes leveraging the time, energy, and resources of others to amass greater riches and wealth.

Each of the money systems must be examined for what they are and leveraged, meaning you must reverse the curse, stop giving away your wealth, recapture cash flow and preserve capital for building lifetime and transferring legacy wealth.

Credit

Credit is a risk, reward-based system used for individuals, companies, banks, and countries. The credit criteria is different for individuals than they are for businesses, than banks, than countries, however, the premise is the same. What is the likelihood of repayment of loan (money borrowed)? If less likely, then there is a lower credit score and a higher interest rate on the loan. The purpose of the higher interest rate is to gain more interest payments (profits to the banks) on the front end, then more principal payments on the back end.

For simplicity, we will discuss personal and business credit.

Personal credit is offered in the form of Lines of Credit (a revolving account with a draw and payback period), Credit Cards (a revolving account with a use, pay down, and re-use monthly cycle) and Installment Loans (loans that can be paid back in short term or long term installments).

Moving from Lack to *Abundance*

In other words, make sure the right motives are in place. Serve people, serve the masses with products that make their life better in an efficient and timely manner. And make sure pricing is comparative or competitive to similar products in the market.

"**GENERAL:**" How have you implemented the Five P's into what you do or how has the Five P's made a difference in your organization?

Demond: #1 At StealthEnomics, we love what we do. We hire people or have teammates who love what they do and would do it for free. So purpose and passion is a criteria of everyone at our company. #2 We seek to meet the needs of small businesses who are launching, building, and growing, providing an 'all in one' shopping experience for eight best steps to get started or to ensure key elements of infrastructure, branding, marketing, and backend support are in place for businesses doing less than $1M in gross revenues. #3 We have business advisors at Family Wealth called Business Strategists who are trained and certified on all of our products. #4 We constantly evaluate our processes and have SOPs (Standard Operating Procedures) in place for creative design specialists, editors, IT support, web designers, admin assistant, hosting, etc. so that we are as efficient as possible. This ultimately helps us scale and handle larger capacity. # 5 For profit, we compare our projections of cost, expenses, payroll, debt vs. various streams of income to determine our Net Operating Income (NOI), from that we allocate percentages for Research & Development (R&D), other capital expenditures and reserves. Our motto is simply: 'We help businesses thrive!!'

"**GENERAL:**" So Demond, am I hearing you say when your staff is purpose driven, mission focused having role descriptions with the right products or

—$ **TAKE BACK YOUR *Wealth!*** $—

Examples of installment loans are car loans with a 5-year-payback period or mortgage with a 30-year-payback period. See chart which denotes the differences below.

LINE OF CREDIT	CREDIT CARDS	INSTALLMENT LOANS
Revolving = Pay Down, Use Again Draw & Pay Back Period Favorable Rates, Higher Amounts Can Be Interest Only, Fixed and Variable Rates	Revolving = Pay Down, Use Over Again Fixed Rate Of Interest Usually 2.5% Of Balance Required Via Monthly Payments	Loan Amount Is Paid In Installments Fixed Or Variable Rates, i.e. Car Loan, Student Loans, Recreation Vehicles, Mortgages

If paying at the banks schedule, it is possible to pay for item or experience a few times over. For example, if a credit card interest rate is 18% because of a 540 credit score (FICO Scores range from 350 to 850, Note: 700+ Credit Scores are great scores) and there is a $3K limit and balance. At a $75 minimum payment required based on 2.5% of the balance owed. It would take 18 years and 5 months to pay off a $3K balance while paying $3,923 in interest. That's a total of $6,923. That's over two times the cost of what was purchased taking close to twenty years to pay for. Ouch!

A person with bad credit scores also falls victim to late fees, over the limit fees, annual credit card fees, etc. Money and wealth are being steadily siphoned away.

Being leveraged by the credit system means paying exorbitant interest rates such as 18%, paying larger down payments and making payments over longer periods of time. To counter being leveraged by the credit system, requires developing the skill set of establishing, maintaining, and prospering from 700+ Credit Scores. We will talk in more depth about

Moving from Lack to *Abundance*

services, it leads to a profitable business? And when having the infrastructure for processing and distribution, delivering products and services in a timely manner, this also leads to a satisfied and a recurring customer base?

Demond: That is exactly right. A recurring and referring customer base helps us to attract, retain, and acquire more customers which leads to increased revenues and profits year over year. Our surplus goes back into Research & Development, better systems, streamlined operations to ensure an enhanced customer experience.

"GENERAL:" You make it all sound so easy, but I know from experience, it takes a lot of talent and skill to manage people, build systems within systems and manage the performance of those systems. Excellent job! That is a word to the wise. Building a business system from scratch is the hardest path possible. It can be done, however, buying into an existing business system with proven practices, operations, and marketing methods is much easier, so you can focus on the customer service aspects of the business. Back to you Pastor Sean.

Pastor Sean: Let's give "General" and Demond a hand. (Everyone applauds). Isn't this learning environment powerful! I often say, there are two ways to learn a foreign language, say Italian, one way is to buy Rosetta Stone or be immersed into the culture. Which method would be more effective and faster in learning to speak Italian? (The audience responds with being immersed into the culture). That is what this environment is like when learning about finance and business. Amen.

this Five Star Success attribute in the next chapter.

Business Credit is oftentimes not discussed in many communities or most do not know how to go about acquiring business credit. Again, it is a risk, reward-based system that penalizes the slow payer and rewards the business that pays before time or on time. There is the Paydex scoring system (from Dun & Bradstreet) from 0 to 100 with 80 or better being considered a great score. Having great scores are not negatively impacted by high balances, as is the case with personal credit cards. When paying invoices or credit cards before due date, it shows that business has sufficient cash flow to pay its bills.

Business credit leads to business funding at decent rates and higher limits than individual loans. Again, the funding can be in the form of credit cards, lines of credit, or installment loans. Business credit helps to apply for loans independent of a Personal Guarantor, therefore not using the Social Security # of the owner. **Warning: if you cannot manage your personal finances and credit, you will have an equally difficult time managing your business finances and credit.** One will affect the other unless having an accountant or tax preparer for the business.

Cash Flow

You may ask what is a cash flow system? First of all, cash flow means volume of (how much) and velocity of (how fast or how often) money comes in or out. Cash flow is also income generated whether actively (i.e. earned or commissioned income) or passively through established systems. The government has a cash flow system from tax revenues at a Federal, State, and Local level. The banks have a cash flow system from fees, interest payments, deposits, and corporations have a cash flow system from products and services being sold and capital being acquired.

Moving from Lack to *Abundance*

UNDERSTANDING MONEY SYSTEMS

Marques is a young man, age 29 who is working as an HVAC Technician. He plans on learning as an apprentice for three to five years to learn the employee role, the manager role, and the boss's role. He wants to study how they hire, how they recognize and reward good performance or behavior. What dues are required, what taxes are paid, what company is used for payroll, where does the company get its parts from? How does it get its commercial contracts? What networking or events take place? What is the training process, what is the promotion process? Marques plans on owning his own HVAC company so he keeps a journal of all that he notices and gleans from his peers, his manager, and the owner of the business. He sees that everything is a system and he desires to reverse leverage all that has been leveraging his time, labor, and resources so he may have more time, resources, and privileges to enjoy his life more, his family, and his pursuits. By being a part of the Family Wealth community, he also understands that there are money systems that must be mastered as well. We witness Marques sharing some knowledge in the workplace during his lunch break.

Peer on The Job: What's up rich boy?

Marques: What's up guys. Why you guys call me rich boy? My name is Marques.

Peer on The Job: Sorry man. We don't mean any harm, it's just you be exhorting knowledge, so we know you will be very rich one day.

Marques: Well thanks for the compliment, but I prefer to be called Marques, okay?

Peer on The Job: We got it. (The others nod in agreement). So what are we learning today Marques? As you can see, you have about five of us interested in what you have to say.

Marques: I'm flattered, guys. You know, you can learn this stuff right along with me. We meet every Thursday night.

—$ TAKE BACK YOUR *WEALTH!* $—

If being an employee only, debtor only, and a consumer only, you will in essence pay too much in taxes, too much in interest, and too much in depreciating or consumable goods respectively.

The counter to leverage cash flow vs. being leveraged by it is to learn how to manage cash flow to pay off debt quickly, minimize taxes and expenses, control spending and preserve estate from taxes and fees through a Trust in addition to a Will. Debt elimination is discussed as a Five Star Success skill set in the next chapter. Trusts will be discussed in Chapter 5.

Business

Business is in short, more than selling something and someone buying. It is more than the number of sales and the amount of revenues per year. There is the structure of a business as a solopreneur or self-employed individual, a partnership, limited liability partnership, master LLP, S-Corp or C-Corp. The structure alone determines the tax advantages, privacy, and protection. There are the roles of sales, marketing, distribution, accounting, research, and development. There is the infrastructure of software apps, merchant services, business credit, etc. There are the strategic partnerships and affiliate relationships with vendors or individuals who have complimenting services, etc. There are SOPs (Standard Operating Procedures) and Job Descriptions for duplication and multiplication.

There is a distinct difference between doing business and building a business. If doing business is the act of selling and someone buying, then building a business refers to building a business system. A business system can be bought into like a franchise or built like an app or real estate leasing company or e-commerce website. Having a business or doing business is vastly different from those who build business systems. Business is an illusion of success. The myth is if starting a business, one can be rich

Moving from Lack to *Abundance*

Peer on The Job: Perhaps one day. I can't speak for the rest of the guys, but I prefer the cliff notes version right now.

Marques: Okay. Today let's talk about the Five Money Systems. Everything is a system. The entire universe is a system that operates off of our beliefs. That is why it's called a belief system. If we recognize a system and use it to our advantage, it will be as the acronym suggests: Save Yourself Time Energy and Money. The Five Money Systems are Credit, Cash Flow, Business, Banking, and Investments.

Peer on The Job: I have certainly heard of each, however what is the purpose of the Money Systems Marques?

Marques: Great question. The purpose of the Money Systems are to move money and make money...also to leverage labor, time, and resources of others to build riches and wealth for the Elite of our society. We are familiar with credit which uses a credit scoring system to determine risk and dependability to repay. There is personal credit we use under the FICO program. That is where the Equifax, Experian, and Transunion credit bureaus came from. Did you know that there is business credit also, administered from Dun & Bradstreet, Experian Business Credit, and Equifax?

Peer on The Job: Man, get out of here. People don't have to use their personal credit in business?

Marques: No, the personal credit should be separate from business credit and credit should not be used for debt but to acquire things that hold or grow in value like equipment, real estate, businesses, etc. not financing clothes, jewelry, a vacation, tools, etc.

Peer on The Job: I wouldn't be able to afford my lifestyle, if I did not use my credit cards for the jazz concerts, the comedy plays, the sporting events, my custom suits, or going on my anniversary cruise with my sweetheart. Furthermore,

and live a life of luxury. The stark truth is, of the 29.5M businesses, 23.8M are considered "non-employers" with no paid employees. The average revenue is around $46K per year before subtracting cost of goods and expenses. What kind of riches and life of luxury can be realized by such revenues and the hours required (typically more than forty hours a week)?

Furthermore, when the business owner gets sick or dies, the business sales often decline or the business dissolves altogether. Seventy-five percent of companies have less than $1M in revenues. The businesses that thrive are business systems that can produce $1M in sales and above per year. They are systems driven vs. people driven so they generate larger and lasting revenues that can be scaled for serving a larger market.

Successful businesses structured as corporations, i.e. S-Corps or C-Corps can offer common stock only or preferred and common stock respectively. Shares can be offered from a private or public company.

The counter to the business illusion is to buy into or build a business system that will give off passive/residual income and is a brand n' demand. According to author Michael Gerber of the E-Myth book series. There must be three roles to form a business system and they are:

Technician—the talent, salesperson, the clerk.

Manager—the person who runs the day to day operations.

Entrepreneur—this person sees and seizes opportunity by setting up and managing business systems.

More will be shared on passive income as a Five Star Success skill set in the next chapter.

— Moving from Lack to *Abundance* —

I had to finance my car and I got to have a new car every three years to get the newest model.

Marques: I hear you, but the only way that works is if you have a thriving corporation writing off the car lease every three years to reduce your tax liability. Otherwise, unfortunately the credit (debt system) got you hooked. Remember this, that the money systems all move money and make money. They leverage time, labor, and resources of others for its own benefit. You and I must counter being taken advantage of and use the systems to our advantage. Begin saving up for the concerts, your custom suits, the sporting events, your anniversary cruises, and pay credit cards off in the same month like what American Express requires or pay off within a three month period at the very latest.

Peer on The Job: Are you crazy? Who lives like that?

Marques: Those who do not want to work all of their lives to pay bills and debt and accumulate no wealth for their future or legacy. That's who.

Peer on The Job: (Slightly embarrassed) I'm listening.

Marques: As far as cars go, some people have 'status anxiety' which is desiring a luxury car like Mercedes, BMW, Lexus, and others. Because cars lose 10% value when driven off the lot and another 10% by the end of the first year, then depreciate on average 15% to 25% each year after that, the rich and wealthy will buy a car three to four years off market with low mileage and dealer warranty and hold onto it for 10 to 12 years, paying for the car immediately or within two to three years.

Peer on The Job: That's going to mess up my bravado. That's a long time to hold on to a car. Why hold on to a car for ten plus years?

Marques: Great question. The truth is that because cars typically lose about

—$ TAKE BACK YOUR *WEALTH!* $—

Banking

Banking is a very sophisticated system made up of the investment side and the commercial side like Morgan Stanley and JP Morgan Chase respectively. Money is made on trades of security instruments, the interest from loans, revolving credit cards and banking fees.

The most profound observation about the banks is how they LEVERAGE, BORROW & BUILD assets over and over again.

The banks leverage cash deposits and convert them to reserves for the purposes of borrowing from the Feds, called the discount rate at i.e. 2.25% (per 2018 info) depending on the banks credit rating. Ninety percent of average reserves can be leveraged(called fractional reserve banking) to borrow from Feds to lend out to consumers and business owners to deposit borrowed funds into their various banks, for the banks to repeat cycle up to 28 times based on the mechanics explained in the Creature of Jekyll Island 5th Edition by Edward Griffin.

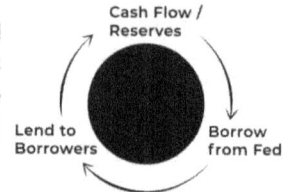

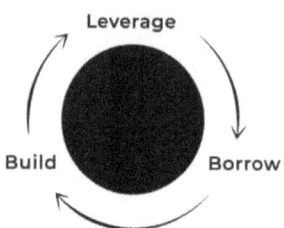

The LEVERAGE, BORROW and BUILD cycle can be done by anyone to go from lack to abundance. The process can be repeated over and over again. Using the model to leverage credit to borrow from bank to purchase investment real estate (build an asset) to leverage home equity to borrow from, to acquire (build) other assets.

— Moving from **Lack** to *Abundance* —

60% of their value just five years in, depreciation doesn't have as much effect ten years out or more.

Peer on The Job: That's a hard pill to swallow.

Marques: Furthermore, if you buy a car toward the end of the year when the new models come out, you can get a better price on the older model still. If you know a wholesaler who goes to car auctions, that will be your best deal possible. That's how you get a car on sale vs. for sale. Credit Unions usually offer decent rates and terms when financing.

Peer on The Job: I never thought about all of that. I thought I was doing something getting my cars brand new.

Marques: Who are you trying to impress anyway? Females? Your guy friends? We think you are already a pretty cool guy no matter what car you drive or how old the car may be.

Peer on The Job: Let me think about it for a while. I have to really examine where the need for a new car every three years is coming from. I may have to have a couch psychiatrist session for that one. (Everyone laughs)

Marques: If you can't save up and pay for it, even a car, you may not deserve it. (He looks around and sees the concerned faces) Let me move on before someone throws their beer at me. The second money system is cash flow. Cash flow is like blood running through our veins. If it ceases to flow, there is a penalty. The government uses tax revenue as cash flow. The corporations use the distribution of products and services as cash flow and the issuance of stocks and bonds for capital. The banks use our deposits as cash flow which is leveraged as reserves.

Peer on The Job: Cash flow is cash flow. What is wrong with that?

—$ **TAKE BACK YOUR WEALTH!** $—

Acquiring and owning real estate is a Five Star Success skill set that will be discussed further in the next chapter. See the numerous applications in the corresponding illustration including those just discussed denoted by an asterisk.

LEVERAGE	BORROW FROM	BUILD ASSETS
*Cash deposits	Federal Reserve	Loans
Credit	Bank Loan	Truck/Equipment
Cash	Secured Loan	Margin Account
*Credit	Bank Loan	Real Estate
Idea	Angel/CV Investor	Invention
Insurance Policy	Bank Loan	Larger Face Value & Cash Savings
*Equity In Home	HELOC	Acquire Asset
Collateral	Secured Loan	Acquire Asset
Cash Value	Bank Loan	Pay Off Debt Or Acquire Asset
Shares Or Stocks	Shareholder	Company Expansion

Investments

The purpose of investments is to make money work to make money for you. Money should be working harder than you and outpace inflation yearly.

There are wealth rules to follow to measure an investment against like a plumbline to sheetrock. There are four rules to abide by. Remember to follow principles first, choose products second.

Moving from Lack to *Abundance*

Marques: If we are workers and consumers only, we will pay too much in taxes, buy more stuff on credit we don't need and deposit and store too much in the bank for the banks to do overnight lending to other banks or to leverage for borrowing from the Federal Reserve (The guys look puzzled). Alright I know I went a little deep, but the bottom line is that our cash flow is king to us so we must preserve it by paying less taxes legally and use it to buy or invest in things that have value, i.e. cash value insurance, gold and silver, real estate, stock and bonds, etc. in that order.

Peer on The Job: Marques, this is like a seminar. The information is no joke. How do you suggest we pay less taxes?

Marques: I don't claim to have all of the answers; however, I have learned that we can adjust our W-4s to ensure we don't overpay the government in taxes in order to get a large tax return during tax season. We can get with our tax accountant and determine how many withholding allowances we want to claim so we don't owe the government and it doesn't owe us. Secondly, we can start by having a home-based business, then build to have a corporation structured type of business like a S-Corp or C-Corp to get more write-offs while increasing our income streams. We can acquire more assets, things that have lasting or increasing value, write off the expenses that pertains to those assets as well as business debt and pay taxes last. When getting businesses off the ground, our start-up costs will reduce our income, therefore reduce the overall tax liability.

Peer on The Job: Have you started a side business Marques?

Marques: I have and guess what it is?

Peer on The Job: What?

—$ TAKE BACK YOUR 𝓦EALTH! $—

1) Preserve Capital (Minimize Taxes, Debt & Expenses)
2) Protect Principal (Do Not Lose Investment)
3) Capitalize On Time (As Time Goes, Money Grows)
4) Compound Growth (Money Multiplies Over Time)

Indexing strategies have become popular over the last twenty years. It was stated in Anthony Robbins book *Money, Master The Game*, how mutual funds (as far as managed funds) are discouraged because of the non-disclosure of fees primarily and how the S&P Index performance alone beat out 70% of the money managers. With fees being as high as 4.52% of the asset value, the long-term growth of mutual funds can be drastically affected. Imagine having the best of both worlds with certain indexed insurance-based products yielding long term safety and growth or indexed related annuity products preserving financial portfolio during the distribution period of life. All wealth principles are adhered to. Safety and growth are key. The Wealth Legacy Plan (WLP) have all key elements included. It would take a combination of term insurance, index funds, bonds, and an annuity inside of a Roth IRA to match the benefits of a WLP and still will come up short.

Imagine having the safety of a savings account, money market account or CD with no losses guaranteed regardless of market conditions and locking in the growth on average (i.e. 7 to 8%) of the market without money being directly placed in the stock market. There are cap strategies which limit growth credited or no cap strategies that capitalize on most of the growth of the market. Both are often used to capture the market performance when there are small gains and large gains respectively while being protected against losses. Gains can be distributed tax free. Consult with a Wealth Strategist to consider a WLP as an effective part of your financial portfolio.

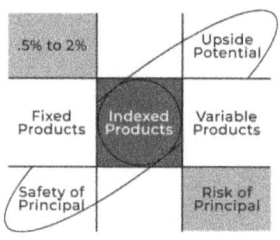

Marques: Helping guys like you get your finances in order, by sharing financial literacy and offering financial products and services.

Peer on The Job: Well Marques, you may have your first clients.

Marques: That would be great. I would love to help you guys. Let's continue with the other three Money Systems tomorrow which are Business, Banking, and Investments.

Tomorrow comes and the same guys plus two more show up eager for more information.

Marques: Alright guys for a recap, what did you learn yesterday?

Peer on The Job: We learned about credit, to use on things that bring more value like real estate, equipment vs. clothes, watches, etc.

Peer on The Job: Hold onto a car for longer periods of time, pay for as soon as possible.

Peer on The Job: Start a business to increase income and reduce taxes legally.

Marques: Okay, good! You guys are on it. Today, let's talk about the other three Money Systems which are Business, Banking, and Investments. When we talk about business at Family Wealth, we refer to a business system, a brand, a business built to scale and built to last. It is not just a business where one or two people sell products, because when the one or two persons get sick or dies, what happens to the business?

Peer on The Job: The business suffers and/or it dies too.

Marques: Exactly! Think about the HVAC company we work for. It is family owned. It has been in existence for 60+ years with multiple locations. The brand or business makes money whether any one of the family's owners are present or

—$ TAKE BACK YOUR $\mathcal{W}$EALTH! $—

✋ There are **Five Asset Classes** and they are Stocks (Equities), Bonds (Loans), Real Estate, Cash and Commodities (Precious Metals). Let's look at each one closer.

Stocks

There is preferred stock and common stock. Preferred stock is purchased at a discount or given to key employees or partners of a C-Corp. Common stock is offered to the general public. There is growth and value stocks. Growth stocks can be high priced to earnings known as P/E (or Multiplier) but the stock price is expected to rise. An example is Walmart (NYSE:WMT) who had per 6/15/2018 a P/E ratio of 18.42 (over 15 can be considered high). Value stocks can be low priced to earnings, however are good for dividends (sharing of company profits). AT&T (NYSE: AT&T Inc.) had a P/E of 12.5 (below 15 is considered low) with dividends yielding 5.4% around January 2018. Dividends can be reinvested to obtain more shares, which are called DRIP (Dividend Reinvestment Program).

Earnings Per Share (EPS) - A portion of a company's profits that is allocated to each outstanding share of its common stock. The formula for EPS = (Net Income/Total Number of Outstanding Shares). Example: If Walmart's net income (gross revenues minus expenses, operating costs and taxes) was $13.64B and shares outstanding (not sold) was 3.1B, then the basic EPS would be $4.40, represented by $13.64B/3.1B = $4.40 EPS. It is one way to determine a company's profitability but is not solely used by itself. If a company like Walmart in this example had a share price of $20 per share, then someone would be willing to pay roughly five times ($20 vs. $4.40) the company's earnings.

not. Because it has been built correctly, it provides passive income throughout a lifetime and beyond. The grandfather who started it has departed and he has his grandsons running the company he started. The company was built to scale and built to last.

Peer on The Job: Building a business to scale and to last seems very difficult to do. Not everyone can build from scratch and there are a lot of hats to wear.

Marques: Yes, that is true. That is why you have to have people around you to bring various expertise to the table. In one of our weekly sessions, we learned how the solopreneur is only averaging about $46K per year in revenues before expenses and taxes while the companies who have employees or partners up to four people average $387K per year and those who employ from five to nine people make over a $1M in gross revenues.

Peer on The Job: Are you serious? Okay, we have eight of us here, yah want to go in business together to make a million dollars? (Everyone laughs).

Marques: Now if you cannot build a business yourself, you can invest into a business system like a franchise where it is a proven model. You and I can buy into an existing business model or build one. Building from scratch is always harder and more risky due to perhaps being a novice and learning from trial and error.

Peer on The Job: What about Banking?

Marques: Banking as a Money System masters the idea of leverage, borrowing and building. It is a powerful model. Has anyone ever heard of Fractional Reserve Banking?

Peer on The Job: No, what is Fractional Reserve Banking?

Marques: Fractional Reserve Banking is when the bank leverages let's say 90% of the cash deposits, known as reserves for borrowing purposes from the Federal

Bonds

Bonds are a form of a loan, an IOU. The purchaser of the bond is the lender and the seller (issuer) of the bond is the borrower. Interest is paid until the principal is paid in full. If a $10K bond is acquired with a 10-year maturity with a 4% annual interest rate, then $400 is paid annually (could be tax free depending on what entity issues bond). At ten years in this scenario, the $10k principal loaned is returned to lender. The most common types of bonds are Municipal, Corporate, and Government Bonds.

Bonds can be used by the issuer to fund long-term investments of projects like hospitals, bridges, roads, or current expenditures like with Government Bonds. Bonds are used to mitigate risk in a financial portfolio when coupled with stocks. Asset allocation is a practice of balancing stocks to bonds based on risk tolerance whether conservative, moderate, or aggressive. A general rule of thumb is asset allocation based on your age minus 100% in terms of mix. See illustration to the right.

AGE	STOCK	BONDS
0-25	100%	0%
30	70%	30%
35	65%	35%
40	60%	40%
45	55%	45%
50	50%	50%
55	45%	55%
60	40%	60%
65	35%	65%
70	30%	70%
75	25%	75%

Moving from **Lack** to *Abundance*

Reserve. The bank lends out to you and I for car loans, home loans, credit cards, etc. at various interest rates. So Fractional Reserve Banking follow the basic rules: only a fraction usually 10% of reserves cannot be leveraged each time. Let me draw this image on this piece of paper. Remember this concept, Leverage, Borrow & Build.

LEVERAGE	BORROW	BUILD
Savings/Reserves	From Federal Reserve	Loan Assets
$100K	$90K	$90K
$90K	$81K	$81K
$81K	$72.8K	$72.8K

Our cash deposits, let's say $100K become reserves which can be <u>leveraged</u>, not used directly to be <u>borrowed</u> against from the Federal Reserve at 90% (of $100K) or $90K then lent out at various interest rates based on the risk of the borrowers for both individual and business loans. The loans are built assets for the bank and liabilities for the borrowers. When the $90K is deposited, it creates an influx to follow the same pattern again and again borrowing 90% (of $90K) or $81K, to lend out to leverage the $81K at 90% (of $81K) or $72.8K to lend out as loans which become assets to the bank to possibly repeat up to twenty-eight times. It is a very sophisticated system.

Peer on The Job: I won't even ask how they can get away with doing that. I will instead ask how can we counter such mechanisms being used from our money to do something similar for ourselves?

Real Estate

There is residential and commercial real estate. There are tax breaks like the mortgage interest deduction and depreciation of furniture, appliances, etc.

The reality is that everyone must live somewhere. Housing is a fundamental need like clothing and food. Owning real estate or buying and selling real estate can be lucrative with 20% plus returns per year.

There are appraisals (comparisons to similar properties within a certain radius of neighborhood). There are inspections for the physical soundness and mechanical functionality. There is a title search to determine title history, any liens on title, etc. There is the deed which is recorded at the county registry.

Title—refers to partial or full ownership or the right to use or modify the property.

Deed—legal document that transfers title from one person or entity to another.

Escrow—Is an account set up for specific distribution on behalf of the owner or interested parties. An escrow account can have taxes, homeowners insurance and /or association dues set aside for distribution quarterly, semi-annually, or annually.

Real estate has skyrocketed over the years. In 1940, the median home value in the U.S. was just $2,938. In 1980, it was $47,200 and by year 2000, it had risen to $119,600 and in 2017, has risen to $199,200. Home values are outpacing inflation and wage growth in two-thirds of the country.

Commodities

Gold and silver are considered hedges against inflation, deflation, or protection against currency devaluation, meaning they have stored value over long periods of time. Gold mining dates back around 7000 years. As

Moving from Lack to *Abundance*

Marques: I am glad you asked. The good news is that there are financial vehicles we are aware of that follow these bank strategies. One is when having equity in the home with good credit scores, the equity can be <u>leveraged</u> to acquire a HELOC, a Home Equity Line of Credit to be <u>borrowed</u> from for <u>acquired</u> assets or the accelerated pay off of debt. Another masterful vehicle is the Cash Value inside of a cash value permanent life insurance policy. It can be <u>leveraged</u> (cash value not touched) to be <u>borrowed</u> against from General Fund to again have paid off debt or have <u>invested</u> for a greater return on investment. The additional cash flow created from either financial vehicle can be put back into the system to repeat over and over again to amass great wealth.

Peer on The Job: Marques, your knowledge base is insane! Are you telling me that the leverage, borrow, and build strategy can be used by me to obtain substantial wealth?

Marques: Yes, that is what I am saying. I will access your financial situation when we meet and show you a unique type of cash value insurance we call the Legacy Wealth Plan because it has comprehensive benefits such as flexibility, accessibility, tax advantages upon growth, distribution and transfer, which we use to imitate the banks beautifully.

Peer on The Job: Yeah, show me. I am tired of living paycheck to paycheck and not having money saved up for my future or my heirs.

Marques: I sure will and it will help you save more effectively. Finally, let's talk about the fifth Money System called Investments.

I will repeat what Robert Kiyosaki's rich dad told him in his Guide To Investing book, *"If you want to invest like the rich and wealthy, you must have 3 E's."* The first E is Education, meaning a financial education. The second E is having Expertise yourself or access to the expertise for what you are investing in and the third is

of 2016, the leading countries who produce or purchase the most gold is China, Australia, and Russia. When gold backed our nation's currency, it kept deficit spending by our government in check.

Without gold backing money, the currency (i.e. paper money) has no intrinsic value (called fiat money). It is only declared legal tender for the purposes of buying and selling goods and services. When the Feds continue to expand money supply (it is like continuing to raise the limit on a credit card) that keeps getting used to the max. Inflation continues to climb which in turn erodes the buying power of the existing currency. The gold standard holds the government to a limit like a debit card. It forces citizens to be more productive in order to spend more. Raising the credit limits are called deficit spending which is *"Simply a scheme for the 'hidden' confiscation of wealth"* - Alan Greenspan, Gold & Economic Freedom, 1966.

Central banks buy gold to reduce risk, support, and stabilize their fiat currencies. Gold is the third largest reserve currency globally after the U.S. dollar and Euro.

Silver is a different kind of precious metal. Because it is historically used heavily in industry. As its quantity of use increases, the price of silver increases. As there is more demand and limited supply, the price increases accordingly. Three high-growth industries are using more silver in production and technology which are self-driving cars, solar power, and healthcare. Technology demands for more silver.

Cash

Cash is simply a currency that is easy to access and convert to its spending equivalent like having money in a checking or savings account.

Moving from Lack to *Abundance*

Excess Cash to work with. Investments require being very knowledgeable about the industry invested in and not following media noise. An excellent newsletter is Stansberry and Associates or Weiss Investments. They have several writers with full time researchers who follow certain aspects of the market. They invest their own money and inform subscribers when to buy, hold, or sell based on a stop loss bottom. My disclaimer is do your due diligence and proceed at your own risk. This information is for educational purposes only.

Peer on The Job: Marques, I really feel like I am at a seminar. Who would ever thought I would get this kind of information on the job. It is amazing you have learned all of this stuff. How long have you been a part of that Family Wealth Community?

Marques: It has only been six months. At Family Wealth, we are taught a lot but are also encouraged to read a lot. That is why I reference so many books. You want to get in the habit of reading because of all of these jewels of knowledge are found within the pages. We have a guy we nickname the General who takes this information and simplifies it for us to embrace and utilize for our greater good.

Peer on The Job: Let's schedule a time for us to go over my finances Marques and give me the time and location of you guys meetings (the others gestured the same).

Marques: I am glad you guys are interested in meeting with me and checking out our weekly meetings. As a community, we are learning five skill sets to counter the Five Money Systems. We call them Five Star Success.

—$ TAKE BACK YOUR *WEALTH!* $—

Large amounts of funds stored beyond emergency fund or savings for future purchases are ill-advised. One reason is based on the devaluation of 'the dollar' affected by higher rates of inflation (cost of goods) and the lower interest rate growth which do not outpace inflation. If savings interest rate is 1% and inflation is 3% per year, then the value of the dollar is losing 2% in interest per year. Furthermore, the amounts stored are subject to being taxable based on its interest growth. If there is 1% interest rate growth on $100, subject to a 25% tax bracket, then 1% gets further reduced to 75% net gain. That is 75¢ net gains on $100 saved. The checking or savings account loses 2.25% in spending power each year in this scenario. In this sense, *"Savers are losers."* **The cash has to be growing faster than inflation** and is best utilized in a tax advantaged environment with no restriction, penalty or permission required.

Cash value life insurance has served such a purpose being accessible, having a faster rate of growth than inflation, and having tax advantages on growth and loans along with the advantage of permanent life insurance. This type of financial vehicle has been used by the Disney brothers, the Rockefellers, JC Penney, bank executives and corporate executives. The cost or internal expenses become minimal after the first ten years because they are not a percentage of asset growth like mutual funds. Financial vehicles like this become fundamental (the first thing that should be put in place, especially with a child) and foundational (what the rest of the financial portfolio should be built upon). Greater strategies leverage policies to borrow from cash value to build more valuable assets (that yield higher rates of returns) and pay policy back.

Building an investment portfolio is how to effectively build lifetime and legacy wealth. You want equity (ownership interest) in these various assets (things that make you money or things of lasting value). Building Equity In Assets become the fifth skill set for Five Star Success living. We will discuss more in the next chapter.

Moving from Lack to *Abundance*

SPREADING THE GOOD NEWS

One week transpire at the Family Wealth Headquarters for the weekly Empowerment & Networking Series. It has been a process of attracting various ethnic groups, religious disciplines, career focuses, business interests, and direct selling industries. Let's rejoin the Family Wealth Community.

Pastor Sean: How is everyone doing? Did you have a great week? (Everyone acknowledges him and nods in agreement). I trust you have. I see we have Kimbell and Nicole here tonight. Thanks for coming out. Kimbell and Nicole are two of our Wealth Strategists. They are a power couple. Amen. Who would like to share what kind of week you had?

Marques: Definitely!! I will share. I had a great week. I am on the verge of having several converts from the job.

Tani: Converts? Are you a minister?

Marques: (Marques smiles) No Tani. Like you, I am a messenger, a Wealth Ambassador sharing the good news of financial literacy and I have an audience at work who are listening and interested in doing better and learning more about how to manage their finances. They are intrigued with the information I have been sharing and want to meet with me for one on one assessments as well as check us out at our Family Wealth meetings. Over the last week, I shared with them the Five Money Systems.

Shaughn Lee: Aviance and myself had a great week too, going over some financial principles with the twin boys.

Aviance: It was great! Our 12 year old boys were very engaged as we talked about the Five Money Rules. The concepts were something they could grasp

—$ **TAKE BACK YOUR WEALTH!** $—

Questions For Review & Reflection:

1) What are the four forces that come against your money?

2) How do you counter the four forces to begin to move from lack?

3) When building a business system for passive income, what are key essentials required for doing so?

4) What is meant by Leverage, Borrow & Build?

5) How can the banking strategy benefit you?

Moving from Lack to *Abundance*

even at their age.

"GENERAL:" Hi everyone. Good evening. Great job Marques for inspiring your co-workers on the job. Shaughn Lee and Aviance, that is fantastic that you are having these financial lessons with your sons. Here are some flyers called Money Success for Children. It shows the Ten Penny Exercise which covers the Five Money Rules and practices the children can do now to develop some healthy money habits. Anyone interested in receiving these flyers? (Everyone raises their hands)

Pastor Sean: Wow Marques, Shaughn Lee and Aviance, you are on fire! Amen. Before we continue, I have to make a special announcement. Besides "General," we have an iconic member of our community who represents Five Star Success. She is typically busy enjoying herself in retirement traveling back and forth to California where her children are. She makes brownies and baked goods for her church and a few organizations she volunteers for. I mentioned a few weeks back that she would be visiting with us on tonight. I am glad to see a full house tonight. She will give us her powerful testimony as to how she reached Five Star Success on her own. She is in agreement with our Family Wealth's Five Star Success Living approach. Her name is Ms. Darla (Pastor Sean looks at Ms. Darla and smiles). Ms. Darla, all are anxious to hear your story, so I yield the floor to you at this time. Let's give Ms. Darla a warm hand clap as she comes up (everyone applauds).

THE ICONIC STORY

Ms. Darla: Thank you Pastor Sean, you are always so passionate about people living out their God given purpose. Your passion is truly contagious. Thank you also "General" for inviting me here

CHAPTER # THREE

PURSUIT OF FIVE STAR SUCCESS

FAMILY WEALTH COMMUNITY
ENGAGEMENT OF CONCEPTS
- Continued -

—$ **TAKE BACK YOUR WEALTH!** $—

GAINING KEY MONEY SKILL SETS

In the last chapter, we discussed the Prelude to Five Star Success, therefore, we covered concepts around financial principles, best practices, and business development essentials.

In this chapter, we will outline the counter leverage to the Five Money Systems. Counter leverage means to flip advantage toward self vs. the elite rich and wealthy who devised the systems. Take back your wealth!

Look at the contrast.

SYSTEM	SKILL
Credit	700+ Scores
Cash Flow	Debt Freedom
Business	Pasive Income
Banking	Real Estate
Investments	Equity in Assets

For proper flow purposes, we will change the order of listing the Five Star Success money skill sets. The proper flow shows when mastering one, it will automatically spill over to conquering the next until achieving all five stars.

✋ The **Five Star Success Money** Skill Sets are most effective listed in the following order:

Moving from Lack to *Abundance*

today and keeping me in the loop with what the community is doing.

Thank you, Family Wealth, for continuing to come together, learn together, and build wealthy families together. Unity is the key to our deliverance vs. everyone operating in their silos losing time and valuable resources through all of the trial and error. So, I salute you for assembling yourselves. When I first heard about the five skill sets that were being taught to counter the Five Money Systems of Credit, Cash Flow, Business, Banking and Investments, I was immediately in agreement.

I am from Nigeria, Africa and spent my adult years in Brooklyn, NY. I got married, had three children and raised them out in California. One of my children moved to Charlotte, NC about five years ago. After visiting with her and her family, I felt my money could buy more and last longer here in Charlotte versus Sunnyside, California. I moved here about three years ago. I am buying a home in cash this year as I had been renting a condo, to get used to the different sides of town and which side would be most conducive for me to settle down for the rest of my life.

How did I learn about Five Star Success and how did I come to achieve all Five Stars for myself? A lot of what I learned came from my father. He was a fisherman in Nigeria and he had a business called "Good Catch." Several restaurants and hotels came to depend on the fish, shrimp, and lobsters his company caught, and he would sell wholesale to the restaurants and hotels. He had a crew of eleven who were very loyal and dependable. When he had to cater to other affairs and not be on site with the other men, they carried on with his right-hand Charlie running the show.

This was my first encounter with business and the concept around creating passive income. There was no credit system like here in the U.S., but there were promises made and signatures representing

—$ TAKE BACK YOUR 𝓦ᴇᴀʟᴛʜ! $—

1) Create Passive Income of $24K+ Per Year

2) Achieve 700+ Credit Scores

3) Acquire & Own Real Estate

4) Eliminate All Debt In Ten Years Or Less

5) Build Equity In Assets Of $200K+

 Create Passive Income of $24K+ Per Year

In our society, we are used to earning dollars for hours and commissions for service. This is called earned income or active income. You must show up in order to be paid. This is very limiting as there are only so many customers or clients who can be helped by you at a time. There are so many hours you can work in a day and there are only so many products and services which can be offered by you alone.

This is why most employees, self-employed or solopreneurs have limited financial success. In essence, MONEY IS BEING MADE TOO SLOW! There is not enough coming in often enough to provide for needs and wants. Furthermore, when facing the forces called Debt, Inflation, Retirement and Taxes (D.I.R.T) or being leveraged by the Five Money Systems, there is no wonder that lack is experienced by the majority of Americans.

Passive income can be created in two ways, one is through investments that pay dividends or lump sums that can be converted to lifetime income. The second way is through leverage of a business system where money is made based on increased quantity and frequency or volume and velocity of products and services sold that can supplement and/or ultimately replace earned income.

If you can master the skill set of creating $24K per year or $2K a month in passive income vs. active income, you will be on your way to mastering $48K or $96K per year. This in turn frees up more time and more money to be used to pursue worthwhile missions or ministry you are purposed for. This is the definition of financial freedom. Want some?

agreement between parties. My father could get fishing equipment, additional boats as he needed them because he always paid as agreed. He paid for our clothes, shoes, food, and daily needs in cash. He never signed for credit on daily needs, only on things related to business. He paid for our home from an owner till he paid it off in about six years. I remember we had a big celebration when he made his last payment. In America, it is called owner financing. Over time he owned his home, his fishing equipment, boats, and other things free and clear.

Upon contemplating coming to America, I was told to find uncles and aunts living in Brooklyn, NY so I did, and I went to NYU for business and finance in the 1970s. I worked at NYNEX Corporate Headquarters on West Street in Manhattan near the Twin Towers after graduation. I met my husband there. During the 1980s, my husband got recruited to Save Mart in Modesto, CA., so we relished more sunshine and warmth. We bought our first home there and we started having children and enjoying our family. I started acquiring real estate quadruplexes (four units in one) and began receiving passive income as a landlord. The flexibility of time worked for me being accessible to my children growing up. Building a real estate portfolio of rental properties helped us to focus on eliminating the mortgages on each one, one at a time till they were all owned free and clear. I kept thinking of my dad saving up to own his home free and clear in six years. I built a portfolio of over $3M by the late 1990s, so I had passive income in excess of $20K per month in the 1990s and still do very easily. My credit ratings have always been high because I kept my personal affairs separate from my business affairs.

"**GENERAL:**" Ms. Darla, allow me to ask, did you have business credit in the 1990s?

Ms. Darla: Great question. No, I did not have business credit, I only used my personal credit for business related purposes. I never used credit cards or personal loans for buying clothes, going on vacation, food, etc. People today can clearly

—$ TAKE BACK YOUR *W*EALTH! $—

Remember this very important quote:

"Money does not have to be earned, money can be created. Trust has to be earned because trust creates money."

- Rodney Archer

Think of the FDIC sticker in the window of a bank. It conveys trust and we bring or deposit our money confidently into the bank. They then leverage our money to create money.

✋ Let's look explicitly at **Five Passive Income Methods** which can assist you with paying off debt faster and simultaneously build more wealth (go from lack to abundance).

The Internet

The internet has become this World Wide Web which can reach people in various countries 24/7. If there is a viable shopping portal or online service accessible by anyone at any time, then money literally can be made in your sleep.

Many people are seeking to offer products on Amazon or Shopify which can yield decent margins and be shipped (or imported) from manufacturer, i.e. China to a fulfillment center for boxing, branding, and delivery. If out of 100 people, any 10 people (10%) use your website to

have a separation of personal and business credit.

"GENERAL:" Did your cash flow fuel everything else?

Ms. Darla: Not only cash flow but converting credit into assets which created more cash flow and repeating that process made life for my husband and I pretty comfortable. Regardless of what assets we had or cash flow we had coming in, we both got life insurance on ourselves for each other's protection, it was a good return on investment. He covered me and the children with health insurance from his corporate job also.

"GENERAL:" What kind of insurance did you get? Term or whole life?

Ms. Darla: We both got whole life because we liked the idea of owning our policy, paying it up at a point in time, having a permanent death benefit, and having access to the cash value if needed later in life.

"GENERAL:" So let's be clear Ms. Darla. Your husband's income stabilized your household and you got into real estate investing for flexibility of time and to add to your household income?

Ms. Darla: That's right. Ricky, my husband, may he rest in peace, was a great provider. We worked well together. We had family meetings to discuss our financial status and progress. When Ricky died in 2003, the insurance policy paid off any miscellaneous business debt and it helped to pay off the children's student loan debt.

From that time till early 2007, I began to sell off properties and place proceeds in a Self-Directed Roth IRA to determine my next set of investments. This is why I say I retired around 2007. My timing was great because the bottom dropped out of the housing market by 2008 and lasted for four to five years. I downsized from the property my husband and I had. I bought a house free and clear and got a Home Equity Line of Credit on the property around 2005. I have two

buy, and they spend $100 minimum, then that is $1,000 in passive and recurring income per month less fees.

Travel internet sites, health or nutritional product sites, feminine hygiene product sites, retail shopping sites, and others have become popular over the years, where the person only needs a replicated website, a specific URL code directed to your own domain (i.e. www.ShopTillYouDrop.com) and a means to drive traffic (or clientele) to your site for recurring purchases via YouTube, social media, Google ads and so on.

Targeting social groups like bowling leagues or gyms, or fraternities/sororities or church life groups or parents' teacher's association, etc. that you are a part of, can be a recurring clientele base.

Real Estate

Real estate is a common passive income stream based on having tenants rent single family homes, a duplex, multi-plex apartment building or hotel. The name of the game is to have as many units as possible with payment frequency as often as possible. Remember volume (how much) and velocity (how often). This is why the game Monopoly suggested upgrading four homes to buying a hotel. Don't we wish it was that easy? However, owning a hotel is ideal because if there are 300 rooms with 50 rooms being rented per day at $100 per day, that is $5,000 per day times 30 days which equals $150,000 gross per month passively.

There is a growing trend around community living properties where a three-or-four-bedroom single family home is converted to a five-or-six-bedroom home with added bathrooms, being fully furnished, having washer/dryer, lights, gas, cable, internet with landscaping and bi-monthly cleaning included. The bedrooms are rented out each week like an Extended Stay Hotel. At $175 or more a week vs. $300 per week (Extended Stay type places), the cash flow can yield around $3,800 per month on average

Moving from Lack to *Abundance*

sons who currently live in the property.

"GENERAL:" You mentioned a Self-Directed Roth IRA, there are not a lot of people who are aware of such an IRA, do you care to explain?

Ms. Darla: Sure, without getting too involved, a Self-Directed Roth IRA gives more control of investments like investment real estate, stocks, bonds, commodities, and even the investment into other businesses directly. The growth in dividends, profits or interest grow tax advantaged and can be distributed tax free as well.

"GENERAL:" Why did you get a HELOC if the property was already paid for?

Ms. Darla: I wanted to be fluid in the event I needed to cover repairs or wanted to make another investment, I could snatch up a deal real quick. Plus, I have my sons paying me so much each month to purchase the home from me. I am owner financing. So I use their payments to pay down the HELOC very quickly. I am not selling the home at market rate. I am mostly teaching my sons how to pay into their own systems, meaning I am taking $300 per month of the $900 they are paying me each to pay into a Wealth Legacy Plan for them and I'll have them continue to pay into it when I am gone. Because it will be their own banking and wealth building system.

"GENERAL:" You are indeed very wise. I have to ask you about this Wealth Legacy Plan you have set up for your sons. Why have you chosen such a vehicle?

Ms. Darla: Remember, I told you my husband and I had cash value whole life policies on each other which paid off in a great way when he died. I didn't think about setting my children up with similar policies, we only had savings to put our children through college. But after meeting you guys at the Family Wealth Community and you showed me how there are more aggressive and safe vehicles to follow people throughout their lifetime, I was sold and wanted to ensure my children have a good financial start. I am setting up Wealth Legacy Plans for my grandchildren also and will pay them up, so the plans can follow them all throughout their lives too.

for a five-bedroom home less expenses, mortgage, taxes, and insurance. That is clearing net profits of $2,000 per month. More people are renting rooms out in their home for passive income purposes too. However, it is highly recommended to have trusted advisors like real estate attorneys and real estate professionals to mentor you regarding the pros, cons, the contracts required and precautions to take in such endeavors.

Business

Business as a brand and a system takes time to build properly, usually three to five years to see some real results or to turn a profit like with a franchise. You have two choices, either buy into a system or build one. Connecting to an existing business system reduces risk because system is already tested and proven vs. building it from scratch.

Building a business system is imperative for true riches and wealth, because the business can be scaled (expanded) to duplicate, to multiply production and cater to more clientele or customers. They take more time, effort, and resources to start up but if built correctly, the business system can afford you more time freedom, more discretionary income, and the ability to pursue worthwhile areas of interest.

"GENERAL:" You are setting up your grandchildren also?

Ms. Darla: Yes, I am, because they have more time on their side to compound growth, I want them to be millionaires in their lifetime. I have taken $30K each and paid up their accounts for ages two, six and nine years old. They will have money readily available throughout their life for college, down-payment on houses, they can pay for cars free and clear, start businesses, pay off all debt themselves and have tax-free income for the rest of their lives after age 60. All without restrictions or penalties.

Pastor Sean: You seem to be pretty excited about it?

Ms. Darla: Well Pastor Sean, you know the good book says to leave an inheritance for your children's children. Furthermore, if there is a catastrophic illness anytime during their lifetime, money can be accessed before death to either put affairs in order or use to protect from drawing down other savings or investments they may have saved up.

Pastor Sean: You are on it, that is exactly our message to the community. Amen.

"GENERAL:" Ms. Darla, you are amazing! Please allow me to steer you back on course. We see #1 passive income of $24K+, #2 real estate, #3 debt elimination, #4 equity in assets of $200K+ and you briefly touched on credit. Did having steady and stable income early on, allow you to have excellent credit scores to get whatever properties you wanted?

Ms. Darla: "General," I will say that having great credit played an important part in helping me build my real estate portfolio. I have to say also, after seeing my sister in law and several other family members abuse credit, that there is a proper order to having and maintaining good credit scores.

—$ TAKE BACK YOUR *WEALTH!* $—

Let's look at the four business systems.

TRADITIONAL	NETWORK MARKETING	FRANCHISE	APPS
Corporate markets and advertises products and services	Marketing and sales are done through networks of people	It is a business in a box, it is usually a standing structure	The apps are downloaded and used by subscribers

Traditional Business

The traditional business model typically will have upper, middle, lower management, and staff. It is corporate owned; therefore, the founder and owner created a passive income machine where the brand is marketed or products are advertised to drive demand and supply. This model requires a lot of skills, knowledge, and the ability to work well with various types of people. The traditional business model typically will employ direct marketing techniques which requires an organization to communicate directly to customers through a variety of media including text messaging, email, websites, online ads, targeted television, radio, newspaper, magazine, outdoor advertising, etc. The goal is to get a direct response from the customer to buy.

Network Marketing Business

The Network Marketing model in its various forms is what has provided a low cost means for you to sell a product or service. This model typically encourages you to use the product or service yourself, invite others to use the products and services and recruit teammates to help you sell the products and services too. You receive recurring income from returning clients and overrides from teammates selling products as well. The upper hierarchy benefits financially from the model because they trained a built-in income stream vs. a future competitor. This model was birthed around the 1930s from The California Vitamin Company rebranded in 1939 as Nutrilite. Two distributors broke off and created their own distribution company called Amway along with other products and services by the

Moving from Lack to *Abundance*

Nicole: What do you mean Ms. Darla?

Ms. Darla: We all know that we should pay on time. Right? (Everyone nods). However, if your income is sporadic and inconsistent, having credit cards can only make matters worse.

Nicole: With all due respect Ms. Darla, people will defend needing credit cards for emergency purposes and justify needing to use them when out of work or income is not as steady or stable.

Ms. Darla: I know that is what we tend to do. However, if you do not have credit cards during tough times, your mind will find other ways to overcome the obstacle. This was my personal experience when I was in college and before my marriage. Money somehow showed up to meet the need without me requiring a credit card to get by.

"GENERAL:" I know that sounds hard to imagine, however I can testify to the same experience. I did not have a credit card and only used debit cards for four years until my income was more steady and then only got one for renting a car or hotel if needed…So Ms. Darla, you used great credit scores to acquire real estate, you used the multiple cash flow streams to rapidly pay down real estate debt which built up equity in the homes. You also had cash value inside of your whole life policies. As it pertains to equity in assets, what other investments did you have ownership interest in like gold and silver, oil and gas, stocks and bonds, or other businesses?

Ms. Darla: I have some gold bullion and silver coins as a long-term storage of value. I have a few index funds vs. mutual funds. I say index funds vs. mutual funds because there are less fees and the performance in most cases have been better. I have a few stocks like Apple, General Electric, and AT&T. I have held

—$ TAKE BACK YOUR *Wealth!* $—

1970s. Due to the explosive growth of product distribution, this business model became copied by thousands of product and service type of companies. In 2013, Network Marketing grew to $178B in global sales and 40% was paid out to distributors. Based on customer (or clientele) recurring purchases and teammate sales production, passive income can be generated. These are primarily people development models, however there is a process of personal development required to be successful. Network Marketing best represents what was expressed by J.Paul Getty:

"I'd rather earn 1% of 100 people efforts than 100% of my own, personal efforts".

You must allow three to five years to master this business model, not just six months to one year as most people do and fall short of their financial goals.

Franchise Business

The Franchise is a business system that has been made 'turnkey,' it is a business in a box like Chick Fil A restaurant or Jan King cleaning services or Mailboxes Etc. and others. This is a proven model. The business is system driven with SOPs (Standard Operating Procedures) where it is plug and play. Plug the people into their various roles and the system produces a recurring income stream. There is a larger up-front cost, so you literally buy into the system.

Phone Applications ('Apps') Or Software Subscriptions

Phone Apps have become extremely popular due to the expected 67% of worldwide population or five billion people who will be using mobile phones by year 2019. The apps are presented for free to get people used to them, then converted to a paying monthly subscription for $1 or more. If having 100,000 people download the app and just 5% actually subscribe, then that is $5,000 per month in passive income from a $2,500 to $10,000 investment (to have app designed and built). Remember when you used to buy software off the shelf, well these days

Moving from **Lack** to *Abundance*

onto them for years. My husband learned about the stock market from a few stock brokers we met in NY when we lived there. We kept in touch over the years. I invested in my sister's restaurant in Georgia and am a 20% stakeholder in that business success.

"**GENERAL:**" Ms. Darla, you have and are living a very fruitful life and make acquiring Five Star Success look real easy. What would you suggest is the best way for people to get started on their quest to achieving Five Star Success or mastering the five money skill sets?

Ms. Darla: Thanks for asking. The order of skill sets are accurate based on how they are listed. (Reading from dry erase board)

1) Create Passive Income of $24K+ Per Year

2) Achieve 700+ Credit Scores

3) Acquire And Own Real Estate

4) Eliminate ALL Debt In Ten Years Or Less

5) Build Equity In Assets Of $200K+

To get started, I recommend having steady and stable income. And learn how to create passive income because it will fuel achieving all other endeavors. Be careful tying up your time with two and three jobs. Keep expenses low. The longer and harder you work for dollars per hour or commissions for service, the more

the software developing companies mostly have monthly subscription services for QuickBooks or Antivirus protection, etc. They want more residual income, more frequently too.

Investments

Investments, once again, can be in the form of stocks and bonds, mutual funds, ETFs, index funds, etc. For stocks, there are growth and value kinds. The value stocks give off regular dividends which can be a source of passive income or be reinvested.

Stansberry and Associates or Weiss Investments are a great source for being informed about dividend paying stocks. Various newsletter writers focus on niche areas of investing. They often invest with their own money and share insights of what stocks to watch, when to buy, hold or sell with stop losses (bottom prices to sell at) built in. All subscribers to the newsletters must take own precautions and invest at own risk.

Examples of dividend paying stocks are General Motors (4.8% yield, P/E 4.06), IBM (3.5% yield, P/E 13.12) and Wells Fargo (3.25% yield, P/E 11.83) in 2016. The payout ratio is one way to determine if a company is a good dividend paying company, which is the following formula:

Payout Ratio = Dividend Per Share/Earnings Per Share

In general, 60% to 80% are reasonable payout ratios. This means for each $1 of earnings, $.80 or less is paid as dividends. Price Per Earning Ratio (P/E) is another indicator of a company's valuation. Price To Earnings of 20 or less in general are known to be a good stock pick. Comparing the ratios from one company to the next is called quantitative analysis.

— Moving from **Lack** to *Abundance* —

taxes you pay and the less options you will have for the future. Let your second endeavor be working to free you from the '9 to 5' or retire your significant other. The second endeavor needs to be an investment into a business or stock that will provide dividend income (which can be reinvested) or a business system like a shopping mall online or vacation portal that your friends and family frequent or real estate leasing or a business that can be bought into or built to scale like a franchise or network marketing business where you are developing people to multiply efforts.

You figure there are at least five ways to create passive income which are investments, internet, real estate, business, or royalties. They are each systems of themselves, so be sure when establishing income streams that you get one system generating $10K to $12K a year minimum before building another. Remember, I focused on building up my real estate portfolio before branching out into other investment opportunities.

Pastor Sean: I told you, you were in for a treat today. What a wealth of knowledge. Let's give Ms. Darla a hand. (Everyone applauds). "General," anything to add?

"GENERAL:" Thank you Ms. Darla for visiting with us today. As you can see, once mastering the five money skill sets, life opens up to more time, more resources, and a higher quality of life. This is why we call it Five Star Success Living. We want all of you to be more intentional to achieve Five Star Success for yourselves and family.

We will do strategic plans with each of you as individuals or families to help you achieve Five Star Success Living in the shortest time possible. We say in ten years or less. We have the blueprint having done it ourselves under ten years to go from zero to hero. If focused and determined, you should accelerate the time frame to arrive at the destination much faster. Let the race begin.

Another method of evaluation used in conjunction, is the qualitative analysis used by Warren Buffett. This method also looks at the quality of management of a company, the brand following (or market penetration) and the product relevance in the marketplace (trending or declining).

Royalties

Royalties are the residual payments to the legal owner from music, movies produced, or they can be licensing rights for book publishing or archived work or use of intellectual property, like copyrights, trademarks, and patents.

If contracted correctly, heirs can receive payments in perpetuity (non-stop, forever), from something produced once. That is a powerful concept.

A great example is Elvis Presley Enterprises (EPE) which includes worldwide licensing of Elvis-related products and ventures, the development of Elvis-related music, film, video, television, and stage productions. EPE manages Graceland and related properties and retail shops. All of this activity continues even though Elvis Presley has been departed since August 16, 1977, over forty years ago.

It is interesting to note that while the general population earns 64% from compensation, the top 1% earns 39% from compensation, 24% from business income and 29% from various investments. The very top of the income scale has 2/3's or 66% of income coming from non-labor efforts.

— Moving from Lack to *Abundance* —

Pastor Sean: You heard it, we are all headed toward Five Star Success Living. What would it mean to you? (The audience shout: Financial Freedom! Having More Options! Spending More Time With Family! Traveling More! Being An Example To My Girls!) Well, guess what? Look around. You are looking at your built-in support and accountability group to help you have it all. Amen. (The people look around smiling).

DESTINATION: FIVE STAR SUCCESS

In the weeks that follow, each individual or family meet with their Five Star Success mentors and coaches to lay out a path from lack to abundance, to go from zero to hero. Let's peep in on some of the conversations and plans.

"GENERAL:" Hi Kimbell and Nicole, you two have been making some bold moves by moving into your mother-in-law's and mother's home to take advantage of her four-bedroom home and rent out your own townhome to free up $2,000 per month. Both of you are getting your insurance license along with Kimbell getting his real estate license. You two are making all of these moves while still working as an engineer, Kimbell, and Nicole you are working part-time as a nurse assistant and raising your three-year-old son.

To achieve Five Star Success, let's examine your opportunities.

Passive Income of $24K+

>You are renting out your townhome at $2,000 per month

> Building a financial services agency around effective tools and strategies, raising up five agents setting up four Wealth Legacy Plans @ $200 per month on average each can yield $6,000 per month in override income per month.

—$ TAKE BACK YOUR *W*EALTH! $—

Achieve 700+ Credit Scores

When having multiple streams of income, starting with active and moving mostly to passive income over time, it makes it easier to establish, maintain, and prosper from great credit scores.

Let it be known as an additional Money Rule to use credit for leverage and not for acquiring debt. In other words, credit cards and equity lines of credit should not be used for obtaining items or experiences, i.e. clothes, appliances, vacations, five-star dining or even car loans or car accessories, etc. If not careful, items financed with credit cards are paid on for years after being consumed, discarded, or depreciated.

Credit should be used for perks and the accumulation of assets that give a greater return than what it's used for. If delayed gratification is employed as a discipline then saving for emergency fund and future purchases can ward off servicing debt. Therefore, the use of credit is for frequent flyer miles, hotel points, shopper rewards based on paying for items or experiences within 30 days up to 90 days max. American Express is not a typical revolving credit card, it is a 30-day credit line that has to be paid back in a 30 day cycle. This requires more discipline and a purposeful use of credit. It is best for small purchases. If carrying balances over several months, then revolving credit cards like Mastercard, Visa, and Discover will be better options for large purchases.

Credit should be used to gain a greater return. A student loan should be obtained if absolutely necessary (Note: A two year or four-year degree may not be required) for the certification or specialized knowledge to be marketable via a career. A credit card can be used for convenience also, like securing an airplane ticket or car rental. Lines of credit are preferred over personal loans due to being revolving.

They can be used to set up margin accounts for trading or for lump sum investments in real estate or stocks, bonds, etc. or paying off debt faster. The income from capital gains, rental income, stock dividends, or

Moving from Lack to *Abundance*

700+ Credit Scores

> With influx of income sources, you can boost credit standing by eliminating any negative items and paying off credit cards and paying off balances monthly to take advantage of frequent flyer miles, hotel rewards, etc. You can leverage the system that has been leveraging you.

Acquire & Own Real Estate

> You already have real estate with more to come, especially since you are a licensed Realtor Kimbell and you got your HELOC before moving out of your townhome. You have conveyed your home over to your corporation for greater write offs and greater asset protection.

Debt Elimination In Ten Years Or Less

> Again, with various streams of income via active and passive income, using snowball method, ALL debt can be eliminated including mortgage, HELOC, car notes, credit cards, and student loans in ten years or less.

Equity In Assets $200K+

> When the house or houses are paid for free and clear, they represent equity in assets. There is the retirement savings in your 401(k), IRA, the cash accumulation inside your Wealth Legacy Plan for yourselves, your parents, and your children. They represent the equity value total of all policies combined. You have equity in your insurance agency and real estate company that will yield wealth when valuated in the future. Therefore, if looking at the chart below…the total equity

cash flow recaptured from debt elimination can pay back or pay off line of credit quickly.

To establish 700+ credit scores, you may have to start with secured credit cards. Secured means that some sort of collateral usually cash in a savings account is used to ensure that credit card is managed responsibly. A line of credit may leverage cash or a title to a car, boat, or equipment. After twelve to eighteen months, the credit card or line of credit can become unsecured and money in a savings account can be released or made available for access again. The credit limits can be raised and usually are raised automatically when satisfactory use of credit has been practiced and established. You can get started at **www.creditcards.com**.

To maintain 700+ Credit Scores, there are **Five Factors That Affect Credit Rating**.

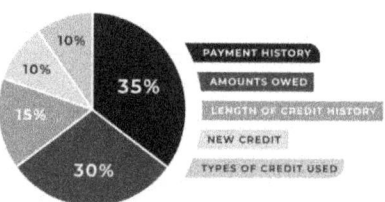

1) Payment History—pay off in roughly twenty-five days (whatever the grace period is) ideally otherwise pay on time. This makes up 35% of score.

2) Amounts Owed—keep credit card balances under 30% of the balance to build credit scores. This makes up 30% of score.

3) Length Of Credit History—have a credit card history for two years or more. This makes up 15% of score.

4) New Credit—limit inquiries about credit history to be done in small periods of time. This makes up 10% of score.

5) Types Of Credit Used—can have a mix of installment loans (at

or net worth of assets are $270,000 to include the $75,000 from your townhome, $150,000 from your retirement vehicles and $45,000 from cash value of insurance policies with much more to come.

Town Home Value	Mortgage	Balance	Equity
$250,000	$210,000	$185,000	$75,000
Retirement Value	Vested		Equity
$150,000	Yes		$150,000
CV Insurance			Equity
$45,000			$45,000

Nicole: The passive income from building an agency is very lucrative. I know how we can set up a minimum of four to eight Wealth Legacy Plans per representative babe (She looks at Kimbell smiling).

Kimbell: How?

Nicole: In addition to the lead generation system developed by you masterminds, you know about the women meetings we have on a regular basis to include baby showers, Mary Kay, tea parties, mom's day out, etc. Almost everyone has children, grandchildren, nieces and nephews and almost everyone desires to have more time and money freedom. They all are women of means and will be standing in line to set up their million-dollar babies or their children's financial future. Everyone loves the idea of being able to 'live forever' in the hearts and minds of their heirs. I'll find five go-getters, who know how to get things done from that group to help us get the message out there.

"GENERAL:" Excellent! I see why you two are nicknamed the power couple. You are making all of these moves while working in your careers.

—$ TAKE BACK YOUR *Wealth!* $—

low to zero percent interest) like car loans, student loans and credit cards. This makes up 10% of score.

*Note: Always remember 61% of credit score is based on credit history and account balances. Pay on time and keep balances below 30%. For more information, go to **www.700scoresfast.com***

To boost scores over 700+, consider some of the proven strategies:

1) Become An Authorized User using a relative's tradeline history without use of their credit card. The relative adds you to their account. They typically will have five years or more history with high limits and balances under 30%.

2) Obtain Unsecured Credit Cards (three max) at $500 or more to establish credit file. Pay off in same month or in 90 days.max.

3) Raise Limits On Credit Cards to offset higher balances. This is called a utilization ratio. If total of all credit cards has been raised to a $10,000 limit (from $7,000) and $2,000 balance remains, then utilization ratio is 20%.

4) Pay Down Or Spread Out Balances under 30% for utilization ratio. Can take advantage of low to no interest introductory rate and transfer balances of current credit cards to a new card, to reduce spread (limits to balances) on the other cards.

5) Consolidate Or Pay Off Balances. Be cautious of consolidating credit card balances and running balances back up. Paying off balances and paying off monthly is best.

6) Dispute, Delete & Settle Derogatory Info so the negative info is taken off or satisfied.

If having less than stellar credit or 700+ credit scores, DON'T SETTLE! Make sure your income is stable (enough is coming in on a regular basis) to handle what you are financing. Repair your credit report to get a fresh

Moving from Lack to *Abundance*

Nicole: Yes, and we have woken up to the fact that our careers won't get the job done for income nor for retirement savings. Both are generated and accumulated too slow.

"GENERAL:" You two got the plan and are well on your way to greatness. Great job!

YOUNG AND STRATEGIC

"GENERAL:" Hi Marques, it is great seeing you. What's been going on?

Marques: I have been helping out quite a few guys on the job set up their Wealth Legacy Plans and they are slowly introducing me to the various groups and organizations they are a part of. They really appreciate me setting up a proper financial base for them and their children's financial future outside of or in replacement of the traditional financial vehicles.

"GENERAL:" Very good! Let's talk about a game plan for you achieving Five Star Success in the fastest time possible. You are saving $200 per month and are now earning an additional $2,000 per month helping others set up Wealth Legacy Plans. Let's translate.

<u>Passive Income of $24K+ Per Year</u>

With lead generation system coming soon, you can mentor and coach three others to make overrides of $2,000 per month plus if you go ahead and buy your first property as a duplex or quadruplex, you can rent out units and live in one of them. If your mortgage is $2,000 per month and you are charging $800 per unit per month, then you are clearing $1,200 in passive income per month minus expenses. You can rent one of the rooms in your two-bedroom unit as well for another $400 per month. I am just saying.

—$ TAKE BACK YOUR 𝓦EALTH! $—

start. You will pay too much for anything you try to do without excellent credit. Do not fall victim to the following traps.

1) Buy Here, Pay Here Car Dealerships With High Interest Rates
2) Title Loan and Payday Centers
3) Monthly Charges On Bank Accounts
4) ATM Charges, Check Cashing Fees, Insufficient Fund Fees
5) Rent To Own Furniture Stores
6) Credit Card Offers In College, In Military
7) Over The Limit Fees, Late Fees

Establishing business credit is recommended for business affairs. Remember credit should not be used for debt but for acquiring a greater return on investment. It is capitalizing on the idea of using OPM (Other People Money) for leverage, borrowing, and building assets. Prove the prototype is marketable and profitable and repeat the process over and over again.

There are four bureaus that track business creditworthiness 1) Dun & Bradstreet, 2) Experian, 3) Equifax, and 4) Cortera.

There are **Five Tiers For Building Business Credit** and they are:

1) Tier 1 - Net 30, 60, 90 accounts, i.e. Shipping supplies, janitorial services, building supplies, etc.

2) Tier 2 - Lower limit retail credit cards, i.e. Gas cards, store credit cards

3) Tier 3 - Higher limit retail credit cards, i.e. Gas cards, store credit cards

4) Tier 4 - Visa, Mastercard, Amex

5) Tier 5 - Lines of Credit and Business Loans

Maintaining 80 or better Paydex scores is equivalent to a 700+ personal

— Moving from Lack to *Abundance* —

700+ Credit Scores

Marques you are at a 640 credit score on average and you have about $7,000 saved up with more to come. I suggest you do two things: 1) Get two secured cards for $500 each, keep balances below 30% on purpose, pay off completely every 60 days. The cards will become unsecured in about a year and you will most likely have a larger credit limit. Also leverage your savings account with the $7,000 in it. Request secured line of credit at your credit union. Leverage account to pay off miscellaneous debt and use income from property and additional income from financial services business to pay back and pay off secured line of credit. You will reverse the curse and leverage the system that has been leveraging you. The purpose of credit cards and lines of credit are not for accumulating debt but for boosting scores and gaining a greater return on investment.

Marques: Roger that. I am completely in agreement!

Acquire & Own Real Estate

Don't just buy a single-family home, you are still young with no family. If Charlotte will be a place of residence for you, then consider acquiring a duplex at minimum or multiplex for greater financial benefits. You can hire a property manager to get the right tenants in the property. We have some excellent Realtors in our community who can help you with that. Convert property to your business entity or Trust. We will discuss in greater detail later. Just let me know if you want me to connect you to a Realtor.

Debt Elimination in Ten Years Or Less

Remember simple rule of thumb, when doubling mortgage payment at 5% or greater in interest rate, it is paid in full in less than ten years. By using a line of credit, you can take $7K savings and increase to $10K for greater leverage. Use it to pay down mortgage at an additional $8K every few months and $2K into saving and investment vehicles. Your discretionary income will help you pay off line of credit every six to ten months to do over again. You are in charge and

credit score. It signifies business cash flow is ample to pay bills on time and is a good credit risk for other businesses to do business with. Using business credit helps to preserve personal credit scores of 700+ credit scores when social security number is not attached to business credit.

 Acquire And Own Real Estate

Since real estate is considered the cornerstone of wealth building and everyone needs a place to live, why not own where you live?

Real estate can be the largest expenditure of any household and if not wise, money, time, and effort can go on seemingly without end to pay off a 30-year mortgage on the banks schedule, paying two to three times what the home is worth. Monthly mortgage payments of $600, $1,000, $1,500, $2,000, etc. can be a burden for such a long period of time.

The first aspect of acquiring real estate is not buying by traditional financing only. There are other ways to acquire a home whether owner occupied (you living in the home) or investment (renting out home).

There are **Five Ways To Acquire A Home**. We will examine all five which are:

    1) Owner Financing

    2) Subject To

    3) Lease To Own

    4) Cash via Tax Liens

— Moving from **Lack** to *Abundance* —

command your cash and credit to go to work for you.

<u>Equity In Assets Of $200K+</u>

As your principal balance is being paid down in your property, you are gaining more equity in the property. If your property is worth $400K, and you've paid down to a $200K remaining balance then you will hit the $200K in equity in assets criteria. We are not even talking about the $10K you have in savings and the investments you will make and the cash accumulation inside of your Wealth Legacy Plan. When you can save up $20K per year and generate $100K plus in income per year, I am going to turn you onto a $3 to $1 premium financing overlay to your Wealth Legacy Plan to exponentially grow your cash value safely for greater lifetime income benefits later in life.

Marques: Wow "General, "this game plan is awesome! I like it. I will get started working on boosting my scores and get with a Realtor and mortgage broker in our Family Wealth Community next. Five Star Success Living here I come.

IT IS WHAT YOU KEEP THAT MATTERS

"GENERAL:" Hi Pastor Sean, I must say I really love your heart for people and your desire to see people have practical understanding of God's word to live a more prosperous life.

Pastor Sean: It is said that information without application leads to stagnation. The Bible says with all thy getting (of knowledge) to get understanding. Therefore, wisdom equals knowledge and understanding. Amen.

"GENERAL:" Amen Pastor Sean. Let's devise a plan. Pastor Sean, you have stable income coming from church salary and your wife's job as an engineer at

5) Bank Financing

Owner Financing

Owner Financing is where the current owner of the home may own the home free and clear. The owner acts as the bank and the principal and interest payments are paid to the current owner. There is a title transfer to new owner with a lien on the title with promissory note used as security instrument in the event of default (not honoring agreement).

Subject To

Subject To is when there is an existing mortgage on the property. There is a Quit Claim Deed transfer to the new owner who takes over mortgage payments or accelerate mortgage payments till paying off loan. The bank has a lien on title until loan is paid in full.

Lease To Own

Lease To Own is when contract is written between owner and lessee, granting the lessee first right to purchase home one year, two, or three years into the future at a set price within appraised values of similar homes to secure financing with so much of monthly payments going toward down payment to purchase. Money can be kept in an escrow account. If lessee refuses to buy, then a portion of escrow is kept as an opportunity loss penalty and an amount may go to the lessee to move out and move on. It is advisable to have a Realtor or real estate attorney

— Moving from Lack to *Abundance* —

Microsoft. You have your construction business that your son now manages. You get offerings from speaking engagements, so you have lump sums coming in and you have some passive income. Can you think of what can help you yield more passive income? There are at least five areas to choose from, i.e. real estate, business systems, internet, investments and royalties from books, etc.

Pastor Sean: I like dabbling in business franchises. I have a mentor showing me how to set up healthy vending machines at several warehouses, corporate buildings, and apartment complexes being there are so many popping up all over Charlotte. The City and County Land Development Departments have proposals for residential and commercial construction. Due to zoning and site inspections, the project must be approved by planning committee to move forward. Once approved, I get a hold of that list from some contacts I have and the construction timeline to anticipate when management will be assigned a few months before receiving their Certificate of Occupancy. I get to talk to management and pitch my vending machines and the additional revenue that can be made for company parties, employee appreciation vendor days, seasonal decorations, etc. while providing a healthy alternative to crackers and chips. We show our satisfaction ratings and income projections and the deal is sold. I can get up to $2,000 per month in no time with about five vending machines installed.

"GENERAL:" It sounds like you got your plan mapped out and it is already working. Is that correct?

Pastor Sean: That's correct. I am feeling pretty good about it.

"GENERAL:" Great! What about your credit scores, where are you?

Pastor Sean: I brought my credit report and I have a 620 with Equifax, a 640 with Transunion, and a 610 with Experian.

"GENERAL:" I noticed you have up to the limit credit cards and late student

assist in drafting up agreements for protection.

Cash

Cash is used primarily when there are tax lien foreclosures. This is when the owner is delinquent on taxes by a few years. The public can bid on property and depending on state guidelines, once tax lien is purchased, the original owner has a period of time to redeem property with bid price plus outstanding taxes and penalty. Property can be acquired for as little as $5K to $15K to $25K, etc. depending on city, state, and county. After acquisition of new owner, the foreclosure process begins to clear mortgage lien from banks if applicable or clear any clouds on title (any discrepancies or other liens). Judicial foreclosures are when foreclosing party such as a bank files lawsuit and requests court to grant a judgment to allow the property to be sold to settle the unpaid mortgage debt.

Traditional Financing

Traditional Financing is based on loan to value, debt to income ratios, decent credit scores, two-year income history with tax returns or bank statements, rental history, etc. The prospective buyer has to apply and be pre-approved then approved for funding.

Lending institutions can finance 100% Loan To Value (LTV) depending on whether borrower is a military veteran or taking advantage of a special lending program (i.e. USDA) or down payment assistance program. There is Federal assisted programs like FHA which require 3.5% down with MIP (Mortgage Insurance Protection) or Conventional Loans with MPI (Mortgage Protection Insurance) up to 95% LTV.

Note: MIP or MPI is required for mortgage amounts over 80% LTV.

Combined Loan To Value (CLTV) is when there is a first mortgage (i.e.

Moving from Lack to *Abundance*

loan payments.

Pastor Sean: I have two kids in college and my student loan from seminary school. I feel like I am mounted with debt because the kids always need something.

"GENERAL:" It seems as there may be some frustration. Do you feel as fast as the money comes in, it goes back out? (Pastor Sean nods his head). There is a wise old man who says, *"If you never live off of what you make, you will never make enough to live off of."* That means, it won't matter how much is coming in, if it is never managed, you will never get ahead whether it is due to higher expenses or more debt. Let's look at your financial worksheet. Your cable bill is $300 and cell phone bill is around $500 per month, your dining out and groceries are $2,000 per month, you have two luxury cars and you are paying over $1500 a month in car payments which you switch out every two to three years not to mention the high car insurance payments for them.

Pastor Sean: When you point them out, it sounds like I may be paying too much out in some areas.

"GENERAL:" That's exactly the way I see it. It is not what is coming in but what is going out that is the problem. You have been blessed with multiple income streams with more to come. However, your stewardship beyond tithes and offerings is off. Are you ready to make some tough decisions and adopt some better habits? (Pastor nods head again). We will need your wife on board too.

Pastor Sean: Okay, I am willing to admit the error of my ways so I may be financially whole, to alleviate the stress and sleepless nights I have been experiencing.

"GENERAL:" That is wonderful Pastor Sean because any organization or family or company or country can progress only as much as the leader is willing to stretch and grow. John Maxwell called this concept, the Law of the Lid. Let's reconvene when your wife is present.

—$ **TAKE BACK YOUR WEALTH!** $—

80%) and a second mortgage (i.e. 15%) preferably a Home Equity Line of Credit. 95% CLTV is usually the max the Fannie Mae or Freddie Mac underwriting guidelines will accept while bringing 5% down payment to the table.

Debt To Income Ratios (DTI) is the housing debt to income ratios to include mortgage (Principal & Interest or P&I) plus homeowners association (HOA) fees if applicable, escrow of property taxes and homeowners insurance (and flood insurance if applicable). DTI also can include car loans, student loans and credit card payments. For example:

DEBT	$2350	
INCOME	$6000	= 39.17%

If gross income is $6,000 per month, and the following information was provided, then the DTI would be calculated as such:

$1500	PITI (Principal, Interest, Taxes & Insurance)
$400	Car payment
$300	Student Loan
$150	Credit Card Payment
$2350	Total Debt PerMonth

43% DTI is usually the highest ratio allowed for a qualified mortgage. There are exceptions up to 55% DTI, however 28% DTI is ideal.

You don't always have to buy a home for sale (retail), you can acquire a home on sale (discount). Connect with Wholesale Realtors, Real Estate Investors, For Sale By Owner, Lease To Own listings and make a deal. You never know what the situation may be that is motivating

— Moving from Lack to *Abundance* —

MAKING MOVES, FEELING GOOD

"GENERAL:" Hi Tani, how's it going?

Tani: It is going grrreat!

"GENERAL:" You sound like Tony the Tiger (smile). Good for you. Today, as you know we are talking explicitly about laying out a distinct plan to achieve Five Star Success in the fastest time possible. You're already making great strides with your passive income which will flow through everything else.

Passive Income of $24K + Per Month

Tani, you have two renters in your four-bedroom, 2500 square foot home. You bring in $2K per month plus $1,200 from military pension and you are involved in Mary Kay for selling and team building purposes. Is that right?

Tani: Yes, that is correct. I do Mary Kay as a way to give back, to help teach others the value of personal development and discipline.

Achieve 700+ Scores

Your credit scores are above 700 plus scores with two of three bureaus. That is quite a jump from the 500's I heard you talk about at one of our Family Wealth Empowerment Sessions.

Tani: Coming out to the weekly sessions as much as I can has helped my thinking and practices using money. Thank you so much. I feel like I am gaining so much to secure my financial future. I am learning and sharing the teachings with my family.

the owner to lease or pass on ownership interest of the property. When seeking non-conventional means, you can have more equity in home, a lower acquisition price, etc.

There are four stages to the real estate relationship and a forward progression required to go from lack to abundance. The majority of Americans never surpass the first two stages. It is time to complete the last two stages to be the true owner (vs. buyer) and wealth builder.

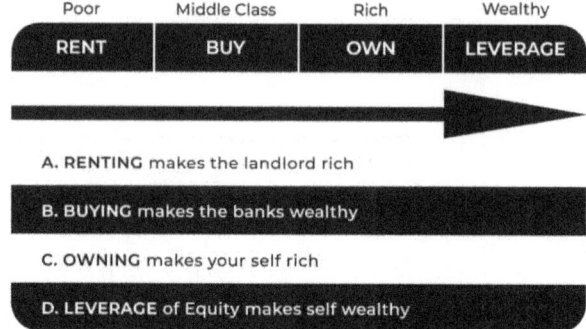

A. **RENTING** makes the landlord rich

B. **BUYING** makes the banks wealthy

C. **OWNING** makes your self rich

D. **LEVERAGE** of Equity makes self wealthy

Renting has a purpose as it is a temporary situation for three to five years max. Oftentimes if you are new to an area, you may want to become more familiar with the new city and learn about the various sides of town before acquiring a home. There are several factors to consider like proximity to work or daycare or school district or older relative or public transportation accessibility before deciding. However, avoid renting as a lifestyle over five years because you can have a harder time making ends meet due to increasing rents year over year. Don't get older and poorer.

The exception to renting is when having a corporation and the lease can be written off as a business expense to reduce tax liability.

Buying a home is equivalent to a "Committed Renter." The often-used term of homeowner is false. The correct term is home buyer. When a home is financed, there is the misconception that you have arrived and are living the American dream. The lure of a home mortgage interest credit is to

— Moving from Lack to *Abundance* —

Acquire and Own Real Estate

"GENERAL:" Tani, you are so welcome. It is my pleasure to teach and my honor to see results in each of your lives. Especially since you have young adult children who are watching and learning from you. Regarding real estate, you bought your home about seven years ago leaving you a remaining mortgage balance of $213K. It was wise to get your son to move into your master suite downstairs for $800 per month and to rent out your upper flat for $1,200 with lights, gas, internet and cable included. That has made a huge difference.

Tani: I know, that is why I am smiling, I can really see a secure financial future for myself.

Debt Elimination of ALL Debt in Ten Years Or Less

Did you know using a fraction of the $3,200 a month you have coming in from passive income, you can pay off your mortgage and any miscellaneous debt in less than ten years? You can get a HELOC for roughly $30K and use as a facilitating account to pay off credit cards in the same month while saving up for future purchases and emergencies.

Tani: I heard a Financial Planner say to an audience to not pay off the home because rates are so low, it is better to earn 8% interest rates with the same money vs. paying off debt at 3.5%.

"GENERAL." This is a great debate! What comes first, the chicken or the egg? In your case, it is important to do both, meaning build wealth and pay off debt simultaneously to prepare yourself for retirement. Paying off debt recaptures your cash flow, reduces your expenses and does not put the home mortgage debt on anyone else when you are gone. If $1,000 of the $3,200 in passive income a month cause a person to pay a mortgage (Latin: death pledge) for 30 years or refinance to keep the payments going for a lifetime. Please note methods of deception: **When mortgage rates are low, i.e. 3 to 4% and there is rapid acceleration of property values, then the people are prone to refinancing home mortgage to pay off credit card debt, student loan debt, etc. for a higher mortgage interest rate of 7% or higher. Without financial education, the unsuspecting borrower runs the credit cards back up to the max and gets stuck with a higher mortgage balance, monthly payment and 30-year debt clock which started over.**

Owning the home free and clear is preferred by other acquisition methods, however if home is financed, it is encouraged to cancel debt in ten years or less to alleviate the long-term responsibility of paying a mortgage and getting in jeopardy of delinquent payments and a threatened foreclosure. Need a tax break? Remember there are five tax strategies to lower tax liability besides a mortgage interest credit. Paying off mortgage and recapturing cash flow makes you rich.

Leverage of equity in the home when mortgage is paid down or there is rapid appreciation in the home is best utilized by a HELOC (Home Equity Line of Credit) vs. a Home Equity Loan or refinancing. The HELOC is fluid like a high limit credit card with check writing and debit card privileges to cancel lingering debt, recapture debt payments, and overpay HELOC to pay off and have for re-use in a few months to acquire more assets. This is how you can make yourself wealthy. Take back your wealth today!

 Eliminate ALL Debt In Ten Years Or Less!

Eliminate all debt in ten years or less sounds like a huge task especially when including mortgages and student loans. Student loans run as high as a mortgage loan being $100K to $150K. However, whatever you focus on expands, in other words when debt elimination is a target, it is easier to focus on.

Debt is one of the four forces (D.I.R.T.) that comes against your finances, so it must first be minimized, then eliminated on the personal side of the

— Moving from **Lack** to *Abundance* —

is used to pay off home with a balance of $213K, the home can be paid off in slightly less than ten years recapturing over $2,200 per month in cash flow. When conveying home to a corporate entity, you can write off depreciating appliances, furniture, HVAC along with write offs for repairs, maintenance, additions, HOA's, property taxes, etc. Check with your accountant and tax preparer to verify and to find out exactly the list of write offs when making such moves. Or I can refer you to someone in our community.

Equity in Assets of $200K+

Using a portion of $3,200 per month for investing purposes can help you build up your nest egg over the ten years you have before you retire. If another $1,000 per month is used to build wealth at 12% average per year, then in ten years, there is about $221,930 or 20% average per year in ten years, there is about $339,113. If home is paid off, then that is over $200K plus in equity and over $200K in investments added to your nest egg for a stress-free retirement when coupled with other cash flow and investment strategies.

Tani: Wow, okay, I will look into setting up corporation and discussing my write off options with my tax accountant. How do I get 12% or 20% returns?

"GENERAL:" There are people like yourself who set up Self Directed IRA accounts with companies like Equity Trust and provide private lending funds to real estate investors to yield 12% to 20% or greater returns per year. The lump sums lent are for rehabbing homes, re-selling, or purchasing tax lien certificates to capitalize on redemption penalties or the ultimate sale of the properties in various states. These transactions occur due to relationships being formed in the community and are not advertised to general public. Real estate is preferred for these types of transactions because the money lent is secured by each property.

equation. It is preferred to use the leverage, borrow and build banking strategy more on the business side of the equation. However, the strategy is equally proficient on either side.

In order to eliminate debt, you must first account for all income, expenses, assets, and liabilities to determine discretionary income and net worth. This information comes from the Financial Worksheet. Again, you can go to **worksheet.familywealthtoday.com** to do the exercise. It is great for individuals, families, and business owners.

Cash flow management is key. In the illustrated example following, you must examine all expenses first. Is there anything that can be scaled back? This exercise is called Minimizing Outflow. The purpose is to limit exorbitant spending in any category to find cash flow that can be redirected toward more worthwhile purposes.

ITEMS	ORGINAL EXPENSE	REDUCTION	REVISED EXPENSE
Cell Phone	$300	$100	$200
Cable	$150	$50	$100
Dining	$600	$200	$400
Entertainment	$200	$100	$100
Shopping	$300	$100	$200
Bank Fees	$100	$50	$50
Totals	$1,650	$600	$1,050

In the illustration, each original expense item has opportunity for reduction. The total reduction frees up $600 per month to have revised expense column total $1,050 vs. $1,650 per month. Now $600 per month can be applied either toward eliminating debt much faster using the roll down or roll up method or building more wealth.

Shifting priorities from obtaining stuff and excessive leisure to ownership and wealth is a mature call. Today and tomorrow are equally important. You should not borrow from tomorrow to live today. Tomorrow will have enough trouble for itself and will need its own supply. Once establishing

Moving from Lack to *Abundance*

BEING AN OWNER & WEALTH BUILDER

"GENERAL:" Hi Demond, listen I really appreciate some of the recent work StealthEnomics did for us with the brochures and stand up banner design and delivery. Your estimate of timing on shipping from printer and stand manufacturer was dead on. Now that's what I call Five Star Service.

Demond: Sure, no problem. You know we have to represent excellence in every way.

"GENERAL:" No doubt. I am a believer. Today, we want to lay out a strategic plan to achieve Five Star Success with your finances.

Passive Income of $24K+ Per Year

You are the CEO and co-founder of your business. You fired your full-time employer two years ago. And you have steady business growth. You have great systems and people in place. You are on your way to having a 'brand n' demand.' You have a Vice President in place handling the day to day operations being groomed to become President of the company.

Demond: Yes, we are making progress. I am giving myself five years to ensure all roles and systems are operating fluidly in order for me to step back as a chairman of the board and receive reports from the CEO of the company.

"GENERAL:" Are you also giving yourself five years to create $24k+ per year in passive income or are you planning sooner?

Demond: I am planning for sooner being I am already two years in, I fully anticipate on achieving a passive income producing system of $24K + in the next year and continue to grow.

—$ **TAKE BACK YOUR WEALTH!** $—

greater disciplines and limits on expenses (spending), it will be time to determine what is called the Debt Accelerator. This is the reduction amount or savings from above illustration that can be re-routed toward eliminating your enemy of wealth.

Here are two examples of eliminating debt. One is a lot slower than the other. Let's look at A vs. B columns with Balance and Payments being exactly the same for the items listed.

ITEMS	BALANCE	PAYMENTS	A EXTRA PAYMENTS	B CONCENTRATED PAYMENTS
CC #1	$3K	$50	$50	$600
CC #2	$4K	$75	$50	$650
Student loan	$30K	$400	$100	$725
Car Note	$15K	$250	$100	$1125
Car Note	$25K	$350	$100	$1375
Mortgage	$100K	$650	$200	$1725
Time It Takes To Pay Off			13.6 Years	7.5 Years

Based on the illustration above, assuming 5% interest rate across all items. When spreading out $600 freed up as extra payments on all six items, Column A will take 13.6 years to pay off all debt. Column B will concentrate $600 to have ALL debt (to include credit cards, student loan, car notes, and mortgage) paid off in 7.5 years. Feel free to do this exercise online at: **https://www.calcxml.com/calculators/restructuring-debt**.

Let's examine this scenario a little closer. When using $600 as Discretionary Income or the Debt Accelerator (DA) in column B and using the snowball method (or roll down or compound method), the mechanics are as follows. The first item being the Credit Card #1 with a

— Moving from **Lack** to *Abundance* —

700+ Credit Scores

"GENERAL:" That is great Demond! What about your credit scores? Are they at 700+ for leveraging purposes?

Demond: As far as 700+ credit scores, I have preserved excellent scores for a while. The reason for this, is because I pay very little on credit cards. I save up for most purchases and more importantly, I separate out my personal from business credit. I buy assets and make moves with business credit and funding vs. my personal credit. I never use my Social Security # as a guarantor for business funding. My Paydex scores and cash flow history helps my business stand on its own merits. I get higher limits, great rates, and I write off more before paying taxes with the business.

"GENERAL:" That is beautiful, you are using the best practices around credit perfectly. What about real estate?

Acquire & Own Real Estate

Demond: My wife and I bought a house three years ago. I expect with all of the activity and sales my company has been experiencing, I will be able to pay off my home in less than five years.

Debt Elimination in Ten Years or Less

"GENERAL:" Again, an excellent plan! Do you know why we stress paying off the home and all debt in less than ten years?

Demond: Is it for peace of mind?

"GENERAL:" That is a big reason, right? The second reason is to own free and clear for equity access purposes. The third reason is to recapture cash flow from monthly payments.

$50 payment, will be paid off in five months, then when adding DA of $650 to the second item, Credit Card #2 with a $75 payment, it is paid off in 10 months, then when adding DA of $725 to the third item, the Student Loan with a $400 payment, is paid off in 36 months, then when adding DA of $1,125 to the fourth item, the Car Note with a $250 payment, is paid off in 42 months, then when adding DA of $1,375 to the fifth item, the Car Note with a $350 payment, it will be paid off in 50 months, and when finally adding DA of $1,725 to the sixth item, the Mortgage with a $650 P&I payment, will be paid off, that is ALL debt will be paid off in 90 months or 7.5 years. Wow!!

While a particular item is being focused on, the regular payments are being made until the debt is addressed. The debt items stand in line waiting to be knocked out (eliminated) one at a time. You now see why we stress that all debt is paid off in ten years or less, with the emphasis on the less. It is possible with discipline and focus. Furthermore, when it comes to credit card debt, seek to consolidate (transfer balances) onto one credit card with a lower or introductory interest rate on transferred amount to help pay down principal faster. You can use an equity line (preferred) or loan to accomplish the same task as well.

Consolidate student loans for a lower or refinanced interest rate to pay off faster. To avoid a lot of student loan debt, seek scholarships and as many grants as possible. Only borrow what is necessary. Work or create income to pay your way through school without acquiring as much debt. Learn how to master creating passive income of $24K or more per year alongside schooling or career to eliminate debt quickly. You don't have to work for public service sector or military to have debt forgiven if you don't want to. You deserve to have choices, however you must be more creative and productive.

—Moving from Lack to *Abundance*—

Equity in Assets of $200K

Demond, because you have primary ownership interest (equity) in your S-Corp structured company…if your company is evaluated to be worth $10M in ten years and your equity share is 60%, then your value is $6M. If your house is paid off in expected time frame, then that is another $350K added to your net worth or total equity in assets. How about becoming a millionaire in ten years or less?

Demond: That's the plan!

LEADERS MUST MAKE SACRIFICES

"GENERAL:" Hi Pastor Sean and Lady Kim. Thanks for coming Lady Kim. As you know, Pastor Sean is losing sleep at night wondering how to rid your household of debt and lack. He desperately wants to experience more financial freedom and surplus. Has it been a concern for you also?

Lady Kim: Yes, it has been a point of discussion a few times.

"GENERAL:" Furthermore, Pastor Sean desires for you two to represent Five Star Success as fast as possible to be an example to your congregation, that favor, and blessings will flow from the head down. Are you in agreement with such a vision?

Lady Kim: I am.

"GENERAL:" That is wonderful. Because there is some good news. You have all you need to go from lack to abundance within 30 days…I'll let that sink in for a moment. (The couple look at each other puzzled). Even though you have two children in college and a lot of expenses, you don't have to carry all of the expenses you have. After reviewing your financial worksheet, you have exorbitant spending with your cable, your cell phone, dining out and luxury cars you trade in every three years.

—$ TAKE BACK YOUR *W*EALTH! $—

For mortgages, seek alternative ways to acquire a home at a lesser cost to pay off faster.

Use 2x Rule: Use 2 times your salary as a limit for buying your home. If you make $75K a year, then the max house value should be $150K.

Double Pay Rule: This is a strategy where if you can afford a mortgage of $3,000 per month, then buy a home where the mortgage is $1,500 and double the payment to pay off in less than ten years when interest rate is at 5% or greater. You don't have to get a 10-year mortgage loan, you can get a 30 year mortgage loan for comfort but don't pay at the banks schedule because you are an owner, not a renter of a mortgage or consumer only. You own items and experiences free and clear as fast as possible.

A HELOC which stands for Home Equity Line Of Credit is leveraged when there is equity in the home at prime + margin (Note: The Prime is set by the Feds for bank lending plus margin which represents bank profits). When having a down payment of 5% or more on a traditional financed house, seek to get a 80% first mortgage and a 15% HELOC 2nd mortgage position at the time of your purchase. The 15% HELOC is like a revolving credit card, meaning you can pay it down and use again. It has checks and a debit card attached to it. Based on the Loan Origination System, the highest the system allows is 95% CLTV (Combined Loan To Value). So if you have 20% to put down on a home, 5% will meet CLTV gap and the other 15% can pay down HELOC which makes the HELOC fluid (liquid) after you close on your home purchase.

If HELOC had a $30K (i.e. 15% of a $200K valued home) limit and was paid down from $30K cash down payment on the home, the $30K will do double duty after closing. The $30K HELOC with zero balance, can be used to pay off Student Loan to free up $400 per month immediately plus DA of $600. That brings the DA to $1,000 to pay back and pay off HELOC very quickly to use again to attack more debt including mortgage. All debt can be paid off even faster in 72 months (6 years) vs. 90 months

— Moving from Lack to *Abundance* —

Let's deal with the luxury cars first and the need to update every three years. You are constantly paying $1,500 per month and you never own the cars, plus you are not classifying the cars for business or writing off the payments or upkeep as a business expense. You two are already prominent members of the community. You have a growing church where you are able to work in the ministry almost full-time Pastor Sean. Is that accurate? Then explain the need for the extra attention? Aren't the cars really no more than reliable transportation? If you are regarded among some of the most respected people in the city, why do you need a status symbol to further denote your accomplishments?

Pastor Sean: Ouch! Get off of our toes. I never thought about it. Perhaps the cars were a gesture to say we have arrived and we are the blessed and favored of God. Amen.

"GENERAL." Would you advise your congregation members to own nothing, accumulate no wealth for themselves or heirs but give tithes and offerings to feel blessed and highly favored? So instead of being empowered to gain wealth and leave an inheritance for their children's children, your congregation follow your lead to have high priced clothes, expensive cars, tons of fashionable jewelry and the latest technology gadgets? Is that what your members are doing, to follow your lead? (Lady Kim lowers her head) Is that assumption correct?

Pastor Sean: "General," you are all up in our home and church man. What do you suggest?

"GENERAL." You know what is coming next, don't you?...Get rid of those expensive cars! Use about $35K and buy two nice slightly used luxury cars for your 'Status Anxiety' and own them free and clear. Put them in the business name and pay yourself back. You be the bank to your business which will pay you back at $500 per month which will serve as a business write off as well. You just freed up $1,000 a month and have reliable transportation to drive. Keep the cars well maintained and hold on to them up to ten years or more.

—$ TAKE BACK YOUR 𝓦EALTH! $—

(7.5 years) in previous illustrated and accelerated example.

If you are already in the home and you have some equity in your home, use your 700+ credit scores to request a HELOC. Inquire from your lending institution or credit union.

⭐ Build Equity In Assets Of $200K+

The definition of equity is simply ownership interest. The definition of assets are simply something of lasting value or something that makes you money.

The Three in One System made up of the Government, Corporations and Banks each have their specialty, such as cash flow, equity and leverage respectively. Equity represents ownership and if you can own it, you can control it without owning it on paper.

Nelson Rockefeller said, *"The secret to success is to own nothing, but control everything."*

✋ There are **Five Layers of Financial Portfolio,** however they must start in a particular order of risk and go up from there. Look at diagram below.

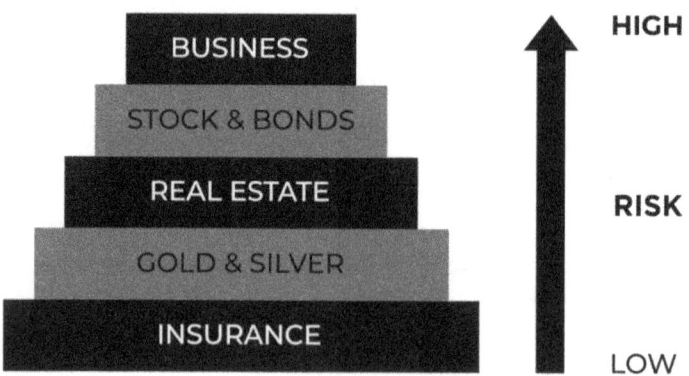

— Moving from **Lack** to *Abundance* —

Lady Kim: The Devil Is A Liar! Do you want us to look poor?

"GENERAL:" No ma'am, not at all. However, will you be poor if you have slightly older cars under warranty that can still be luxury cars to satisfy the 'Status Anxiety' many of us have? Do we need to take a break?

Pastor Sean: Continue please. We are in a little shock right now, but we'll take the medicine. Amen.

"GENERAL:" Lady Kim? (She nods to proceed). Second, $2,000 a month for dining out. Is that including the children in college? Is that entertaining other pastors, ministers, or special guests each month? Is it a personal chef? Are there other members of the household beside your youngest and you two? What am I missing? I am only seeking to better understand.

Lady Kim: It's just us three and the children when they come home from college or the eldest who runs the construction company, stopping by from time to time.

"GENERAL:" Why is so much being spent?

Lady Kim: I don't cook often nor does Sean, so we probably spend $60 to $70 a day on eating out.

"GENERAL:" And that is not including groceries, do you realize that? What if you had a chef prepare a variety of dishes at $40 per day or $200 a week. That will save you almost $1,000 a month. Between the cars and food, you will have an additional $2,000 a month. If you took some cooking classes, you could eventually reduce costs more. I hope I suggest these things and still be loved. (The couple smiles back and nods in agreement)...Let's talk about the $300 a month cable bill, why is it so high?

Pastor Sean: I don't know, we don't even watch TV that much. The bill has been increasing over the years perhaps due to some special promotion we take advantage of and don't cancel. We're just use to paying bills, I guess.

"GENERAL:" Pastor Sean, don't you oftentimes say, "The people have a debt

–$ TAKE BACK YOUR *W*EALTH! $–

Insurance

In Robert Kiyosaki's book *Guide To Investing*, Robert pointed out two very important points. He said, *"Insurance is a very important product and needs to be considered as part of your financial plan, especially when you are first starting out."* Furthermore, it was stated that 97% of people never become rich because of their priority or order of choices. It is amazing that the Rockefellers used cash value insurance and Trusts to preserve, grow, and transfer wealth for generations vs. the Vanderbilts as told in the book, *What Would The Rockefellers Do?* James Cash Penney used cash value in policy to meet payroll and day to day expenses. Walt Disney borrowed from his to help finance his theme park, Disneyland. Ray Kroc used his to cover salaries and marketing campaign for mascot Ronald McDonald.

It has been determined that cash value permanent life insurance is foundational. It should be the base for which your financial portfolio is built upon. It should be formula driven and will simply build wealth over the long term with little to no risk.

Cash value insurance policies should be set up on the children, the grandchildren, and great grandchildren, this means the parent, grandparent, or great grandparent should start them. There is a cash value accumulation which is equity built up in a long-term asset that can follow a child all throughout their lifetime, not just till college. It has more accessibility without restrictions, penalties, or permission being required before age 59.5. It is useful for borrowing for school expenses, buying a car, having a down payment on a home, paying off debt, leveraging to start a business, and having a lifetime income stream tax free (depending on how it's set up). There are enhanced plans that have even more features and great growth with downside protection besides. They are called Wealth Legacy Plans.

Other types of insurance include term insurance, disability insurance, health insurance, home, and auto insurance to cover the what if's and unexpected circumstances around your health, car accident, disability,

Moving from Lack to *Abundance*

consciousness vs. a wealth consciousness?" How do we change it? Do we start with the heads of organizations and families?

Pastor Sean: Absolutely, I am ready to do my part. I mean we are ready to do our part. Isn't that right Queen?

Lady Kim: Yes, we will do our part.

"GENERAL:" With alternatives to cable TV such as internet streaming, there is Amazon Prime, Hulu, Roku, Sling, and Netflix which cost a fraction of what cable TV costs. So you should be able to comfortably save $200 per month. Lastly, there is the cell phone bill of $500 per month. What is going on?

Lady Kim: We have cell phones for six of us and we lease the phones and three notebooks, so we can have free upgrades on the technology each year if need be.

"GENERAL:" I understand that you have your entire family on the phone plan and like to stay up to date on the latest technology. If you bought the notebooks outright as business expenses, could you hold on to them for about three years?

Pastor Sean: Yes, we can do that.

"GENERAL:" What about owning a few phones that come with the plan free and clear and leasing only a few? I saw family plans for six up to $250 per month with no contract. Even if we add another $125 per month for leasing, that is $125 savings per month. Change family plan into a business plan for the expense write off as well. Are the adjustments worth it?

Pastor Sean: (He looks at Lady Kim, she nods) Yes, it is worth it. We can do a lot better.

"GENERAL:" Okay, so we are up to $2,325 per month saved in 30 days if you take action. With that savings, consider the following:

1) Pay yourself first, allocate $700 per month for you Pastor Sean and $500 for you Lady Kim due to male rates are higher than female and you are little older Pastor Sean. That is $1,200 per month total. Set up your Wealth Legacy Plan

death, burglary, fire, natural disaster, and negligence in some way.

Term insurance has a place, meaning it is purchasing protection in the event of death to replace income, pay off home, put children through school, etc. It is renting coverage for a specified period of time (10, 20, 30 years) to perhaps build up wealth in the interim to replace coverage. The reality is for most using this strategy, *"Buy Term and Invest The Difference,"* it did not serve the American people well over the last 40 years. Without financial education, the people were relegated to traditional retirement vehicles like 401(k)s and IRAs and 95% of Americans ended up with no wealth and no financial protection in their elder years. Don't gamble with your life, covert term products to permanent protection as soon as you can especially if younger. It will help you save and accumulate cash, have bundled major illness benefits and multiple tax advantages as a base level of protection and wealth preservation.

The use of health and disability insurance, home, and car insurance are to assist with capital preservation of your money if a major incident occurred. However, seek to pay the least premiums possible with health insurance by having an accompanying Health Savings Account for high deductible and copay plans. HSA's are for saving up for qualifying medical related expenses while benefiting from tax advantages. Disability insurance premiums can be lower when electing for longer disability waiting periods due to having emergency funds saved up to cover you for six months or longer. There are health share programs (it is not traditional health insurance) like Liberty Health Share with low monthly premiums for individuals, couples, and families. The program works best for proactive health conscious people. Shop around for best rates on bundled home and auto insurance each year. Your zip code, your credit scores, your distance to work, your age and driving history or claim history can affect your rates.

with those amounts to protect against the cost of becoming ill, dying too soon and providing income later on in life.

2) Begin to pay down credit cards at an additional $500 per month to $1,000 per month to boost scores and continue onto paying off mortgage too using snowball method to increase equity. Take a minimum of $10K and allow your investor friend to show you how he sets up and manages his online trading accounts, especially if he is having 20% or better returns on average. That is impressive to build up your financial portfolio to again increase your assets. So as a recap, in order to reach Five Star Success in the shortest time possible, you can do the following:

Passive Income of $24K+ Per Year

You have the vending business, construction business, and pay from the church to achieve $24K+ in passive income, right?

Pastor Sean: That is correct?

700 + Credit Scores

"GENERAL:" When you're paying off your credit card debt quickly and you pay off each month, your credit scores will increase. Take $10K that's sitting in your savings and leverage it as a Secured Line Of Credit for the $10K margin account via online trading account for investing purposes. It is another form of leverage, borrow and build assets. Use the higher returns to pay back Secured Line Of Credit quickly. If borrowing at 3% and earning 12% to 20%, the account will be easy to pay back and your scores will increase.

Acquiring and Owning Real Estate

Gold & Silver

It was stated before how these precious metals are a hedge against inflation because they hold intrinsic value. They are a true form of money that can be traded all over the world in the event of a collapse of the current fiat (I owe you, based on the belief of people) money system. Having ownership is a form of equity.

There are a lot of sources from mining companies to domestic and international companies who offer gold and silver by the coins, by the grams, by the ounces and so on. There is the purity to consider and the storage of them once received. More knowledge is required to avoid the risk of being scammed. During the year of 2000, the lowest price for an ounce of gold was $264. That same ounce of gold today (5/19/2018) would be worth $1,295 which is almost 5x the investment in growth.

Real Estate

When a property is owned free and clear, the equity is available for use. It is how you can have your own banking system to leverage the equity to build more wealth. The faster mortgages are paid down, the more equity there is. Please note, before you convert an owner-occupied home (a home that you live in) to an investment home, PULL THE EQUITY OUT! This means take your 700+ credit scores and acquire a home equity line of credit preferred (vs. equity loan) for access to the equity. You can have up to a 95% LTV HELOC on owner occupied vs. 60% to 80% LTV (Loan To Value) for an investment property.

Real estate can help you speed up your portfolio if you know what you are doing with buying and selling, fixing up and flipping, wholesaling (hypothecating—finding a deal and having an investor to buy) or investing in a REIT (Real Estate Investment Trust). Having the expertise or connecting yourself to the expertise can yield 12%, 20%, or greater returns on your money. Setting up a Self-Directed IRA can give you more options and your own discretion of investments in a tax deferred environment. Equity Trust is a well-known Self-Directed IRA (or Roth IRA) company.

— Moving from **Lack** to *Abundance* —

You two bought your home a few years ago, so now you will use several income sources to pay down principal balance to gain equity and recapture the cash flow of the monthly mortgage payment. Also, use income from children who may come back home to live for a while after obtaining their college degrees. You will ensure both of you have a place to live for many years to come.

Debt Elimination in Ten Years or Less

Since debt is the enemy of your wealth, using the debt accelerator calculator I told you about, you can have all debt cleared in definitely less than ten years. Let's do the math using the debt accelerator calculator and $750 minimum as Debt Accelerator. The website is **www.calcxml.com/calculators/restructuring-debt**.

ITEM	BALANCE	INTEREST RATE	MONTHLY PAYMENT	MONTHS TO PAY OFF
Credit Card #1	$5,000	7%	$75	7 Months
Credit Card #2	$6,000	10%	$100	13 Months
Student Loan	$15,000	5%	$150	26 Months
Student Loan	$7,000	5%	$125	30 Months
Mortgage	$180,000	4.25%	$1050	116 Months

Pastor Sean and Lady Kim, all debt can be paid off in 116 months or 9 years 8 months freeing up $2,250 per month. How's that?

Pastor Sean: That's awesome! I feel better already.

Equity in Assets of $200K+

"GENERAL:" When eliminating the home mortgage and the value of the home is $225K, that is $225K in equity you can leverage with a HELOC for building more asset value. You have 51% ownership in the construction business and if you sold the business for $2.5M, then your equity in asset value would be around $1.3M. You also have 100% equity in the online trading account and cash value of insurance to make your net worth pretty sizable over the next few years.

—$ TAKE BACK YOUR *W*EALTH! $—

Stocks And Bonds

Having shares or stock is like having ownership interest or equity in a company. The shares represent value. When buying low and selling high, this is called capital gains. It is also called trading for which stock brokers get paid to do. There are day traders who use Ally Invest, Ameritrade, Scottrade, ETrade, and several other online trading platforms, where there is no minimum required to open up to $10,000, with per trade amounts being around $3 and up. Brokerage accounts can be set up also, where the investor deposit funds with the firm and place investment orders through the brokerage to buy, sell stocks, bonds, mutual funds and the more advanced investments such as currency, futures and options contracts. Whether trading yourself or hiring a brokerage firm to do so, it can be very risky timing the market as 70% of money managers get beat by the "market" (S&P 500). If leaving it in for the long term, annualized average returns not adjusted for inflation or taxes have been 11.69% from 1973 to 2016.

Business

A traditional business is invested in where you have ownership interest as a member (a silent partner) or managing member (an active partner), it can yield both profit sharing as having a salary or a dividend paying schedule. Building the value of the company over the years is where the wealth payoff can occur. A business system can be the most lucrative of all, especially when experiencing 30%, 50%, or 100% growth year over year or growing a business from $1M in gross sales to $2M to $4M etc. year over year.

However, the skill sets required to build a business from scratch are enormous and requires years of mastery. Owning a franchise or proven direct marketing business or online platform or vending company, etc. reduces the risk of failure. However whatever choice can vary in startup costs. A business can take three to five years to turn a profit from investment made. It can take less time if having a mentor and a proven model to follow.

Moving from Lack to *Abundance*

BEING INTENTIONAL WITH EVERY MOVE

"GENERAL:" Hi Shaughn Lee and Aviance, you two have definitely been aggressive, leasing out both sides of your two-bedroom duplex.

Passive Income of $24K+ Per Year

You recently moved out of your five-bedroom home and turned it into a community living home, renting out each room and fully furnishing the house and providing cable, internet, lights, and gas. You are bringing in $800 from each side of the duplex. You anticipate having your community living home fully occupied in just a few months with the potential to cash flow at $175 per room per week times five people; that is about $3,800 per month. So, $1,600 plus $3,800 will equal $5,400 in passive income per month so far.

Aviance: Since Shaughn Lee loves managing and maintaining properties. I picked up another business venture, selling things on Amazon. My last products were Bluetooth headsets around Christmas time and I have three others that I keep in stock and get sold on a regular basis. That business is now bringing in $1,500 per month. As I am mastering my craft, I can get it up to $5,000 a month over the next year.

700+ Credit Scores

"GENERAL:" Wow, you two are doing it! When looking at your credit scores, Aviance what are you doing to boost your scores?

Aviance: I am paying my credit cards off in the same month. As a matter of fact, I primarily use my debit cards or cash for day to day purchases. So I either have it to spend or not. Shaughn Lee definitely keeps his credit score high and he has great practices that I am imitating.

—$ TAKE BACK YOUR *WEALTH!* $—

Building equity in assets is the same as net worth, which is the value minus cost or asset minus liability. When reducing liability or debt, the more assets you can own free and clear, the more you can build lasting wealth and abundance throughout your lifetime.

The Five Star Success or Five Money Skill Sets are essential for reversing the ill-effects of the Five Money Systems. When mastering the Five Stars, then the levels of sophistication can be added on top for creating more passive income, using more business credit vs. personal credit, buying and owning more real estate, living debt free, and acquiring over $1M of assets (and wealth) in a lifetime to pass on heirs. This is how it should be.

Acquire & Own Real Estate

"GENERAL:" That's great! You two work well as a couple and you hold each other accountable to your goals and daily practices. Congratulations. You have three homes. You have the duplex, the community property, and your residential home. Being that your passive income is increasing with rental income and the Amazon business, your passive income outside of your jobs are totaling $6,900 per month and your mortgage payments are what?

Aviance: The duplex mortgage to include principal and interest payments is $1,580/month.

Shaughn Lee: The communal property is only $1,259/ month. I bought the home at the bottom of the real estate market in 2011. We have the $50K HELOC we pulled out before moving to our new home. We used it towards our down payment on our new home and we have a HELOC as a second mortgage on our new home as well. That was ingenious using that strategy. We have two HELOC's worth $50K with interest only payments. Our new residential home principal and interest payment is $1,384 per month. We currently have all of our investment homes conveyed to a business name so we may have more expense, upkeep and furniture depreciation write offs too. The business is the first insured and myself and Aviance are the second insured on homeowners insurance policies.

"GENERAL:" I see you two have gotten pretty sophisticated.

Shaughn Lee: We are not playing. When we learned about the leverage, borrow and build banking strategy and how the Five Money Systems seek to leverage our time, talent, and resources for its own means. We decided we were not going to be pawns any longer. We were instead going to become players at the table with a knowledge of the money rules and exercise all options to win the game.

—$ **TAKE BACK YOUR WEALTH!** $—

Questions For Review & Reflection:

1) What is Five Star Success, meaning what are the five money skill sets required to go from lack to abundance?

_____

2) Where are you as it relates to Five Stars, do you have one, two, three, etc.?

_____

3) How many would you like to achieve and by when?

_____

4) What will be your passive income system? And when will you get started?

_____

5) What savings and investments do you have? Is it enough or are they performing as desired?

_____

— Moving from **Lack** to *Abundance* —

<u>Debt Elimination in Ten Years Or Less</u>

"GENERAL:" I am curious to see how all of your debt including three homes can be paid for free and clear in ten years or less.

Aviance: Let's do it! We don't have any other debt. Our cars are paid for. There aren't any student loans or tax liens or judgments, etc.

"GENERAL:" You two remind me of an engineer by the name of Dameon, who took the information provided and began making major moves and went from 2 Stars to 4 Stars in 8 months. He hit all 5 Stars in less than two years from the time he received the information.

Shaughn Lee: I remember you talking about him at one of our Family Wealth Empowerment sessions.

"GENERAL:" Alright, let's do the chart. We will use 80% of $6,900 to account for vacancies, repairs, and fluctuation of income which is $5,520 in net income per month. Your active income from your jobs are paying the

CHAPTER # FOUR

PROSPERITY OF FIVE STAR SUCCESS

FAMILY WEALTH COMMUNITY
ENGAGEMENT OF CONCEPTS
- Continued -

—$ **TAKE BACK YOUR 𝓌ᴇALTH!** $—

BUILDING A PROSPEROUS COMMUNITY

Community leadership must consist of dedicated persons who each have a role in creating a Five Star Success Living environment. When there is structure and order, there can be duplication and multiplication across the country. Four vital roles are necessary to ensure the community spreads the message, educates, disciples, and inspires members and coach aspiring and expanding business owners.

The four roles are as follows:

Wealth Ambassadors are persons who are messengers of the good news around financial freedom and legacy wealth. They can be a...

> Host or Hostess of live or virtual events, gathering people for the occasion or inviting people to existing events or webinars.

> Financial Educator, therefore certified by the National Financial Education Council (NFEC) or equivalent program to teach financial curriculum to others.

> Group Presenter, who speaks in front of various groups and organizations across the country.

> Group Organizer, who brings others together who are like-minded to establish a community in the approved city.

Ask yourself how you can help us get the Wealth Movement message out to the world. Could you be a Wealth Ambassador?

Wealth Strategists are licensed and certified professionals in the areas of life insurance and other disciplines in the financial services industry. Other licensed designations can be in the health, property, and casualty insurance space, estate planning, legal profession, taxes, and accounting, real estate, mortgage lending and financial planning as it pertains to securities, investing and cash flow management.

— Moving from Lack to *Abundance* —

$1,384 mortgage payment in your new residence property. So, $5,520 plus $1,384 equals $6,804. Take total net income of $6,804 minus total mortgage debt of $4,573, that equals $2,231 per month as a Debt Accelerator. When listing everything accordingly and using the accelerated methods, all three homes are paid off in 102 months or 8.5 years. Is that pretty impressive? Using the Debt Accelerator and calculator, the results are shown on the chart following.

ITEMS	VALUE	BALANCE	% RATE	PAYMENT	PAYOFF
HELOC #1	$50,000	$50,000	4.0	$350	21 Months
HELOC #2	$50,000	$0	4.25	$0	n/a
DUPLEX	$225,000	$175,000	3.5	$1,580	59 Months
COMMUNITY PROPERTY	$250,000	$180,000	3.1	$1,259	84 Months
RESIDENCE	$235,000	$185,000	4.25	$1,384	102 Months
TOTAL	$810,000	$590,000		$4,573	102 Months

Shaughn Lee: You got me a little teary eyed seeing those kinds of results. What in the world have I been doing over the last twenty years with all of the money I have made? I am just glad Aviance and I can correct a ton of mistakes and really enjoy our lives and build wealth for our future and generations to follow. We are thankful!

Equity in Assets of $200K+

"GENERAL:"

You two are so welcome. My heart is warmed by seeing the light bulb come on and you wake up to how powerful you really are and what you can accomplish in your lifetime and beyond. So from the same chart, you already have over $200K ($810K—$590K = $220K) in equity, not even including your 401(k)s on the job or the cash value you are growing for yourselves and the twins Wealth Legacy Plans. You are well on your way to becoming millionaires and examples

—$ TAKE BACK YOUR 𝓦EALTH! $—

Business Strategists are those who are experienced or willing to be trained consultants for helping others in the community launch, build and grow sustainable business systems that will yield passive and active income streams with the emphasis on the passive, recurring or residual income. Business owners are guided in the following areas of business development:

1) Structure and Formation
2) Product and Service Discovery
3) Brand & Technology Development
4) Patents, Trademarks & Copyrights
5) Setting Up Manufacturing, Ordering, and Distribution Systems
6) Marketing & Advertising Campaigns
7) Cash Flow Management, P&L Statements, Projections
8) Market Penetration & Customer Retention
9) Corporate & Staff Team Building
10) Selection Of Board Of Advisers
11) Business Credit & Funding
12) Equity & Bond Positioning

Wealth Builders are comprised of members of the community who have vowed and committed themselves to achieving Five Star Success. They are customers utilizing effective tools and strategies who serve as powerful examples of how lives can be greatly enriched when employing the Five Star Success blueprint.

When this ecosystem is built and working properly, certified representatives of Family Wealth are called upon to speak to various types of organizations in numerous cities across the country. Communities are formed with key positions to educate, empower, and enlarge territory of financial literacy and financial freedom.

Moving from Lack to *Abundance*

for others to be inspired by...Why are you smiling **Aviance**?

Aviance: I never imagined being a millionaire in my lifetime and I never imagined it being so easy to accomplish. It appears to be a matter of having the insight, the information, the execution and the discipline to walk the plan all the way out. Once the routine is established, it only needs to be duplicated and multiplied to get even greater results. It is really amazing to see; all of this is happening to me. (Looking at Shaughn Lee) I mean for us. I am very happy!

ACHIEVING MORE, LIVING BETTER

Fast forward five years later, the Family Wealth community has grown leaps and bounds, the people feel hope, they are firing their jobs (or making opportunities for others to fill their roles on their previous jobs) and have become true crusaders.

Shaughn Lee: Welcome everyone to Family Wealth. We are a community of like-minded people addressing our economic dilemma going from lack to abundance. We have grown tremendously and have truly started a revolution with our books, online curriculum, media, jingles, radio show, short story films, infomercials, mascot, children books, etc. Look around the room. We started with about twelve of us and we have grown to over 2000 members locally and hundreds of thousands who watch via live stream. We have over 200 Family Wealth Chapters across the country and over 50,000 members who are made up of Wealth Ambassadors who share information and invite people to our various events or curriculum. We have Wealth Strategists who assist people with streamline game plans to be financially secure and wealthy in their lifetime and beyond. We have Wealth Builders who are customers and examples for others to follow and we have Business Strategists who help others build their businesses to scale and to last.

Many of us who joined the cause five years ago, are financially free today crossing

Trusted advisors are adopted by each member of the community to make more informed decisions and go through the process of denouncing lack and embracing abundance forever.

CHANGING OUR WORLD

Imagine, if you will, an entire community of organizations and people achieving Five Star Success. Do you think life for yourself would be more rich, more enjoyable, and more fulfilling with less stress? Do you think more good could be done in the world, more giving could take place and more people could be impacted by your organization?

Then, if you and I agree that life could be lived being well and doing good, then why not create the world we would like to see? Let's first start with ourselves, then the company, organization or church each of us are a part of or have influence in.

> *"If you don't like it, change it. If you don't see it, create it."*
> —Rodney Archer

This is why Family Wealth was formed, it is a group learning environment where a community of like-minded individuals denounce lack and declare a life of abundance for themselves, their children, and their children's children. That is powerful right?! Think about Mayer Amschel Rothschild who established his banking business in the 1760s. He spread banking internationally through his five sons who established their presence in London, Paris, Frankfurt, Vienna, and Naples. Today, the family's interests have spread into financial services, real estate, mining, energy, mixed farming, winemaking, and nonprofits. It is estimated that the family's net worth is $350B and controls more than $2T in assets. So, it proves that a lasting and enduring empire can be created from the ideas and intentions of one person. That person is you and I.

Moving from **Lack** to *Abundance*

over to the other side to abundance vs. lack. This was due to the information, tools, and strategies being taught and learned and applied. We had to keep the vision of Five Star Success in front of us because they were skill sets that were measurable and trackable. We were motivated by reversing the leveraging of the Five Money Systems, focused on the practices of the Five Money Rules, strategic with the Art Of War and we pursued Five Star Service levels with the businesses we were and are still building to create multiple streams of income via passively and actively. We constantly stay in tune with our mind, will, and emotions around money for it is a means to an end and not the end of the matter itself. Money is a servant and not our master. Our needs are met in abundant supply, so we may meet the needs of others. This is why we were and are here, to enjoy the fruit of our labor and to help others along the way.

We are not an island to ourselves having to figure it all out on our own and only fend for ourselves. We are a group of people who are now playing life, finances, and business as a team sport. We all have our roles and if we will play them well, we can win more times than we lose. We have concluded that if we have time freedom, money freedom, good health, love and the freedom to pursue purpose and passion, that is real wealth.

Member of Family Wealth: Shaughn Lee, you, Mr. Kimbell, Ms. Tani, Pastor Sean, Ms. Darla and others are icons now in only five years. You all caused a financial revolution to occur, what was the catalyst?

Kimbell: We stand on the shoulders of giants (the masterminds) who envisioned changing the financial landscape for millions of Americans. They made the sacrifices for years being assured that the outcome would ultimately be as they had envisioned. We credit "General" as we affectionately call him and his dedication and those who he gleaned from via books, through live mentorships and his experience as well. Today, you have the blueprint, the yellow brick road that was laid for you to go from lack to abundance. We proved the blueprint works and there is another side waiting for the masses to enter into.

—$ **TAKE BACK YOUR WEALTH!** $—

✋ So what if this Family Wealth Community could come alongside **Five Types of Organizations** which are:

1) Social Organizations

2) Professional Organizations

3) Charitable Organizations

4) Financial Organizations

5) Educational Organizations

The plan would be to have an online curriculum with accountability and coaching from Wealth Strategists and Business Strategists who could help people streamline their path to Five Star Success and stay on target until reaching their goal.

Let's look at the prosperous potential for each organization.

Social Organizations, i.e. fraternity, sorority, bowling league, skating, softball, flag football, hiking group, etc. Let's fast forward under ten years with the majority of organization members achieving Five Star Success. More dues are paid, more often, more participation would occur more often, there would be more volunteers, more equipment and more resources made available for organizations to do more for its members, more often, do you agree?

Professional Organizations, i.e. National Sales Network, Business Network International, Chamber of Commerce, Latin Chamber, Corp. of Engineers, SCORE, etc. When more career professionals like attorneys, accountants, doctors, engineers, and others learn how to create passive income to replace earned income, there won't be a need to sacrifice 60 to 80 hours a week to earn a living. More people can carry the load especially if more people are only serving their profession for ten years max. There would be no need to work 30 years in order to retire. One could have multiple careers or passionate pursuits in a lifetime. Sounds great, right?

— Moving from **Lack** to *Abundance* —

Shaughn Lee: Remember ideas are things. If you and I can express and present those ideas, others will fund those ideas. That is what happened when the national financial curriculum was birthed. It was funded, built, launched, and presented to organizations across America. The lessons being taught on a weekly basis became accessible and available to the masses. Between the book, audiobooks, and online curriculum, the mindset changed, then the habits, and then our lives. I, Kimbell and many others are the products of the transformation of information to manifold manifestation in our lives. I will share the comparison between when Aviance and I first started and where we are today. The other pioneers in this space will share their stories as well.

Before we started coming to the meetings, each of us ran our finances separately, only contributing from our separate bank accounts. I would take care of so many household expenses, via mortgage, HOA dues, taxes, maintenance and Aviance would take care of the cable, internet, groceries, electric, gas, etc. We never really talked about finances as a family. I focused primarily on school work with the twin boys. So, as a household, we had scattered resources and all I knew was that I was over 40 years of age and needed to prepare for retirement and Aviance needed to save more. We both were facing some anxiety about our future, because even though as an engineer, I have been paid very well, I still did not have much to show for it in the way of lasting wealth for my future and beyond.

After I started attending Family Wealth meetings, I would share the lessons weekly with Aviance. Eventually, she was so intrigued with the information, she started coming out more regularly. After a while, we started having weekly financial lessons with the boys from the two-sided flyers we were receiving, and the information became more accessible after the online curriculum got launched.

—$ TAKE BACK YOUR 𝓦EALTH! $—

Charitable Organizations to include the Muscular Dystrophy Foundation, the Cancer Society, Samaritan's Feet, Fishes & Loaves, Goodwill, Salvation Army, churches and other foundations, etc. Giving has been consistent over a 40-year period of time from 1976 to 2016 being at or above 2.0% of GDP (Gross Domestic Product). The donations come primarily from individuals vs. corporations or bequest or foundations. This is wonderful even in lieu of 95% of Americans who may be broke or still working at the age of 65. This proves that it feels good looking out for the needs of others vs. catering to ourselves only. When Americans carry less debt and have built more wealth, charitable donations can exponentially increase all the more. When the masses adopt and are able to comfortably give 10% of gross income to a worthy cause or causes, then more clothes, shelter, food, and humanitarian goodwill can be given. Remember the Money Rule: Give 10% To A Worthy Cause.

Financial Organizations are credit unions, credit card institutions, banks, for profit and non-profit credit repair organizations, mortgage modification companies, real estate companies, accounting firms, estate planning firms, etc. Back in the 1920s when the Richest Man In Babylon book was published, it was distributed free of charge by the banks to the savers, so they may learn to deposit 10% or greater of their earnings into the bank for access if needed. Today, when people have access to pertinent information to give them a better handle on their personal finances, they can be more successful regarding establishing business systems. They can better leverage their cash flow, credit or collateral (assets) to borrow from the banks to build more assets (things that have increasing or lasting value). When repeating this process for various reasons as noted on page 72, the banks win due to more loans and the

Member of Family Wealth: So you and Aviance began to get on the same page and discuss finances more among yourselves, then that grew to having weekly family lessons?

Shaughn Lee: That's right. There were two lessons that were profound for our household. One was having a joint checking account agreed upon for household expenses and a joint savings account for our agreed upon planned vacations, repairs or purchases, etc. Our personal saving and checking accounts were for the following:

> Savings #1 - is for paying myself first, preserving a minimum of 10% for long term wealth building purposes and Savings #2 - for saving for future purchases or events and handling emergencies with the car or family, etc.

> Checking—for paying personal car notes, student loans and credit cards off each month. The checking account is for transferring funds to the joint account for additional expenses or savings also. So, this is what it looks like on the whiteboard.

Shaughn Lee Accounts	Joint Accounts	Aviance Accounts
Income	Transfer	Income
Savings #1	Checking	Savings #1
Savings #2	Savings #1	Savings #2
Checking	Savings #2	Checking

You can go to **familyplan.familywealthtoday.com**

businesses win because they are able to scale (handle larger capacity) and distribute more products and services.

Educational Organizations that include financial education in parochial, junior high, high school, and colleges as well as trade and technical schools bring valuable life money skills to its students.

"An Academic Education Is For Helping People Earn A Living, A Financial Education Is For Helping People Build Lifetime & Legacy Wealth."
—*Rodney Archer*

It is not how much is earned, it is how much is preserved. Therefore, with more money wisdom, more people can make ends meet and make money last and multiply in their lifetime. Learning community economics like what the Hispanics, Asians, Jews, and other ethnic groups do can provide more housing, food, clothing support, so no one family has to go it alone. With a financial education, there can be less reliance on welfare, food stamps, and government subsidies and more interdependence with other families and communities instead.

EARLY DISCIPLINES

Teaching children early can create helpful financial habits throughout life, like a simple exercise we at Family Wealth call the Ten Penny Exercise. It can be done at the schools as an exercise and lesson to the kids or at home with each child.

Set up five jars (or five envelopes) with five labels. Each week, parents

Moving from Lack to *Abundance*

Member of Family Wealth: Wow, that is simple but organized. I should have been doing something like that myself. I will have a talk with my wife this coming week. Thanks.

Shaughn Lee: Yep, when we first wrapped our head around the concept, it made sense immediately. Especially since we set our personal budgets and contribute to the joint account based on a percentage of our individual pay. The second lesson we learned about was truly separating out our business accounts from our personal, so we set up a Family Trust as the owner of the businesses and Land Trusts or Partnership LLCs or Self-Directed IRAs for the real estate we own and a S-Corp for the business entity we run. We have separate bank accounts for each linked to QuickBooks. The accounts sort accordingly:

Accounts	Business #1	Real Estate #1	Real Estate #2
Merchant Services	Income	Income	Income
Checking	Expenses & Debt	Expenses & Debt	Expenses & Debt
Savings #1	Reserves	Reserves	Reserves
Savings #2	Taxes	Taxes	Taxes

Member of Family Wealth: Why a LLC for real estate, a S-Corp for business and a Trust as the Owner of it all?

Shaughn Lee: Great question. There is no one size fit all answer when it comes to LLCs, S-Corps or Trusts. There are many other structures to consider depending on what is being set up and why it is being set up. I suggest you talk to our Business Strategists or Wealth Strategists with estate planning expertise for the best scenario in your situation. All entities provide a level of privacy and lawsuit protection for the individual or families acquiring assets.

—$ **TAKE BACK YOUR *WEALTH!*** $—

or grandparents gives child ten pennies (or ten, one-dollar bills). A teacher can demonstrate the Ten Penny Exercise in classroom each week with enlarged toy pennies, Monopoly money and oversized jars.

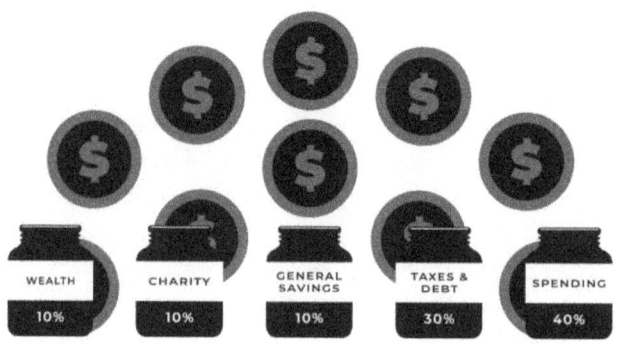

OUT OF TEN PENNIES:

One Penny should go in the Wealth Building Jar.

Money Rule: *Pay Yourself First, Preserve 10% Of All Your Pay.*

One Penny should go to Charity Jar.

Money Rule: *Give 10% To A Worthy Cause.*

One Penny should go to General Savings Jar.

Money Rule: *Save For Emergency Fund & Future Purchases.*

Three Pennies should go to Taxes & Debt Jar.

Money Rule: *Minimize Taxes And Debt, Then Reallocate.*

Four Pennies should go to Spending Jar.

Money Rule: *Manage Spending With A Plan.*

Have child save to buy candy, toys, etc. for 25 cents, 50 cents, $2.00, $10.00, etc. without going into the Wealth Building Jar, Charity Jar or Taxes & Debt Jar. Money Rule: *Practice Delayed Gratification & Saving Disciplines.*

They can also reduce tax liability as corporate structures as well as perpetuate inheritance transfer advantages. The important factor to consider is to always have a clear separation between personal and business and a clear separation between businesses and real estate.

Member of Family Wealth: That is wise!

Shaughn Lee: Kimbell, do you care to share your story.

ADVENTURES OF KIMBELLMAN

Kimbell: I would love to; however, I will ask my lovely wife, who is here this evening to share.

Nicole: Okay. Hi everyone. I am a true convert to Family Wealth and I am so grateful for the amazing group of people we are connected to and the community we are building. Initially, I was very skeptical about Kimbell joining up because I thought it was another direct marketing company, except the product was not a juice, lotion, or a potion, cell phone or energy product, it was financial services. So, my mind immediately went to a well-known company out of Atlanta, GA with a direct marketing distributing and team building model. What was different about this venture, was Kimbell's enthusiasm didn't wane.

After three months of activity, going to Family Wealth Empowerment sessions and trainings and sharing what he learned with the two-sided flyers, notes, and challenges. He started talking more about money and wealth principles and how we should be handling our finances. Now ladies (looking at the ladies around the room), you know we crave stability and security. I started to pay attention when my man was talking about financial security for us in the future and jumpstarting our son's financial future. It all made sense to me and there was 'no pie in the sky,' 'swing for the fences,' 'once in a lifetime investments' talked about.

—$ **TAKE BACK YOUR WEALTH!** $—

Each week, have child give One Penny out of Wealth Building Jar to parent or grandparent in exchange for Two Pennies in return. Have child return both pennies to Wealth Building Jar. Money Rule: *Invest To Grow Money.*

And/or let child know for every amount they have accumulated in Wealth Building Jar every three or six months, the amount allocated will be doubled. Then double the amount for them. Do this as long as you can. Money Rule: *Capitalize On Time And Compound Growth.*

When the children are older, move them to saving accounts for same disciplines and margin accounts for investing purposes. This exercise becomes a habit that leads to prosperity in Five Star Success Living.

When a community can connect to organizations all over the country and cultivate an empowerment atmosphere (suggested by Dr. Claud Anderson of Powernomics) among constituents of that organization be it leaders, individuals, and families, all can go from lack to abundance in a shorter time span.

THE EDUCATOR, COACH & GUIDE

When there is an online curriculum that contains three steps to helping people achieve Five Star Success starting with 1) Transforming The Mind to think and act like an owner and wealth builder, 2) Transitioning The Position to move from a lack state of being (living paycheck to paycheck) to a surplus existence (having time and an abundance of resources) and 3) Transferring The Wealth for later in life to live off of and for generations to build upon. So in addition to the content, there is a scoreboard tracking the Five Star Success achievement where organizations and their subscribers (supporters) can be compared to other organizations and their subscribers as well and individuals can compare their start times and star levels to others starting around the same time. Everyone is moving toward the same destination in a friendly competitive environment.

— Moving from Lack to *Abundance* —

He showed me a proprietary product called the Wealth Legacy Plan which had protection against downside losses and potential of upside gains that could follow us and especially our son throughout a lifetime up to age 120. I was impressed that it did not have restrictions, or penalties like a 401(k). When he showed me how we could help our son be a millionaire in his lifetime, I was sold hook, line, and sinker as they say. Ladies, you know how we love our babies and our children (all of the ladies nod in agreement) and desire to give them the best life has to offer. Setting up our son for financial success throughout his lifetime was the least we could do. I thought about the countless women who feel the same way, especially when having means to do so. I decided to join forces with Kimbell and my respect level for him soared when seeing the caliber of people at the Family Wealth events.

When he would put on his suit coat, I began to see him with a cape instead. I began to nickname him Kimbellman. Kimbell worked hard, he got up super early in the morning, he worked out, helped me with our son, went to work for 9 to 10 hours a day, then met with people to assist them with their finances, spoke in front of various groups and would seek to be home by 8:00 pm at the latest to spend time with our son and myself. Even today he gets started early in the morning, working out, meeting with people and groups sharing the good news of Five Star Success Living.

People are so hungry for a different lifestyle, that when we have seminars or invite people out to these Family Wealth events across the country, the places are jam packed. Look around the room, do you see what I mean? Kimbell goes and goes and is absolutely drained late in the evening, because he ensures the same passion and attention is given at home too. I am truly blessed to be married to a superhero. I have these headlines on the mirror in our bedroom. One headline came from him having our three-year-old son on his lap and both of them were asleep. The headline read…

—$ **TAKE BACK YOUR WEALTH!** $—

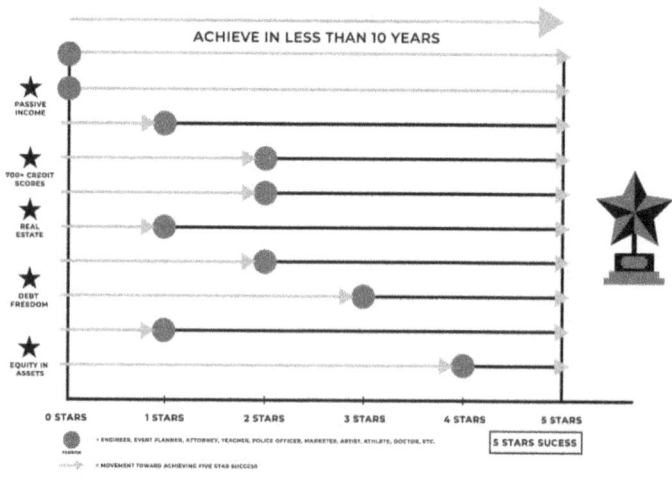

In the book Richest Man In Babylon, the King of Babylon wanted its citizens to learn how to be rich so he may have the richest and wealthiest city in the world. That deserves repeating, the concerned monarchy desired for its citizens to be educated in the area of finances, so all may live well and the city may be recognized for its cleverness throughout the annals of time. Shouldn't the aristocrats of any society do the same? The idea around an online curriculum is so the information shared in this book may be accessible for the masses with tracking and accountability to reach the destination of Five Star Success. It will be a subscription base and organizations will receive 25% of monthly subscription payments as a means to empower its supporters and receive additional resources for its own purposes. Once the base skill sets are mastered, then duplication and multiplication of the same will help to elevate the people to an entirely different level of living, as it should be.

There is an opportunity for organizations to be first in line to be contacted for beta testing of the online curriculum. If interested, you can inquire

Moving from **Lack** to *Abundance*

"HERO BY DAY, FATHER BY NIGHT"

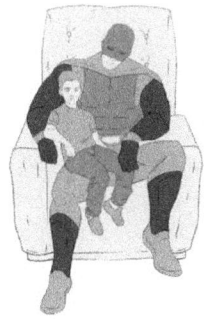

Another headline came from when he declared that we were to be financially independent in two years. He exclaimed how he needed to fire his boss and make room for others who needed a work opportunity. I was ecstatic to see our income increase passively and actively to the point of replacing $200K per year. We were and are having the times of our lives, traveling as a family and speaking at various venues and all kinds of groups, churches and organizations across the country. I called the headline…

"LOCAL HERO TAKES CONTROL"

—$ TAKE BACK YOUR *W*EALTH! $—

at **organizations@familywealthtoday.com**. We are Coming Together, Working Together, Learning Together, and raising up Wealthy Families/Communities Together.

BUY AND BUILD WEALTH

There is a fundamental financial vehicle that can be used for all Five Star Success skill sets. At Family Wealth, we call it the Wealth Legacy Plan. It can create passive income tax free in a person's elder years of more than $24K per year especially when started early in one's life. There just needs to be enough time to build a sizable nest egg to be converted to a lifetime income stream. Each person can create their own program, tax free outside of 401(k)s, IRAs, 403(b)s, 457s and Social Security dependence. Teachers, Firefighters, Police Officers, and Government Employees can use such a powerful tool to supplement retirement income to ensure not running out of money from age 60 up to age 120.

When using debit cards to pay as you go or paying off credit cards within the grace period (of usually 25 days), larger purchases like an automobile can be purchased with the Wealth Legacy Plan. The concept is called Buy and Build Your Wealth simultaneously. Your 700+ credit scores can be preserved once established because you become your own lender reversing principal and interest payments from the banks, creditors, and lenders back to yourself. So instead of obtaining financing from the financial institutions where the money paid never comes back to you, if you acted as your own bank, the lender to yourself or loved ones, then you recapture 100% of your principal and interest payments for continuing to build your wealth.

Let's slow down to help you grasp this concept. If there are five cars bought over a lifetime at $30K each with $5K in interest charges over five years, that is a total of $175K ($35K x 5 times) paid out in cars over

Moving from Lack to *Abundance*

Allow me to share one more instance and headliner with you. Early on, when we moved into my mom's four-bedroom spacious home to care for her more closely and to convert our townhouse into a rental, he found out she had purchased a new car with a five-year note. He was outraged and expressed his concern to me, he said, *"We will carry no more debt in this household! We will build our assets and let our assets buy our luxuries free and clear!"* I agreed, so we convinced my mom to return the car. Within a five-day period, Kimbell drove the car back to the dealership with me and my mom following in our car.

Member of Family Wealth: You were able to take the car back up to five days? What did they say?

Nicole: Yes, that was correct. Now, please know that it is not standard by any means. Typically, there is no 'Cooling Off' period except in cases of misleading or non-disclosure of certain facts. The car was politely returned and accepted. We ended up finding a car just as nice, slightly used which we snatched off the lot with our Wealth Legacy Plan and my mom is paying back into the plan. We are our own bank. I teased him once again with the headliner:

"KIMBELLMAN SAVES MOTHER IN LAW FROM DEBT SYSTEM"

a lifetime to never return to your bank account. Correct? Now if you had your banking system and you purchased the cars free and clear from your Wealth Legacy Plan, you would pay principal and interest back to yourself each time, therefore building wealth of $175K while purchasing five cars in your lifetime. You own the item or experience free and clear. Sounds too good to be true? These strategies have been used by the rich and wealthy for decades if not centuries. These types of maneuvers do not involve credit at all, and can be paid back at your leisure because you are the owner of your wealth building account.

Need a down payment for a home or want to purchase a tax lien certificate or judicial foreclosure in cash, to own a home free and clear? You can make a five-minute phone call and have a check mailed to you within three business days. You don't have to employment qualify or reserve qualify or credit qualify. You don't need permission and there are no restrictions or penalties or tax consequences before age 59.5 if understanding the guidelines and proper funding of your Wealth Legacy Plan.

If you are your own bank and if there is lingering debt, all debt can be paid for in ten years or less. If employing other money rules and practices, your Wealth Legacy Plan will have ample amounts to cancel debt rapidly and you can pay yourself back with no hassle, no collection calls and no amortization schedule.

You can also use saved up amounts for making one-time investments in hot stocks or targeted ETFs to enjoy greater returns to repay Wealth Legacy Plan. The interest earned on investments can be in addition to the average 7% to 8% compounding inside the plan itself. You can also lend to your children for their wedding, car purchases, home down payment, etc. and give them an amortization schedule and promissory note to pay back over a specified period of time. You become the lender, however when the children pay back the loan, they pay back into their own inheritance. Wow!!

Kimbell: All I can say is when having my wife as my partner in agreement and working with me on our crusade, I feel like a superhuman. And over the last five years we have been able to do some extraordinary things. We have built teams and communities of people all over the country to spread the good news about us all going from lack to abundance. Marques, do you care to share next?

NEW POSSIBILITIES

Marques: Man, where do I start? All I know is that I appreciate you introducing me to the Family Wealth Community. I have learned so much and am living life at a totally different level. When I joined the Family Wealth Community, I was working in the HVAC industry and was seeking to own my own company. I did that and started doing warranty work. I grew my business to three independent contractors and I made some money, but it was not as rewarding as helping people set up their Wealth Legacy Plans. After I got my insurance license and started helping some guys on the job with their overall finances, it was great to hear how much more their lives was fulfilled securing their own financial future and jumpstarting their children's.

I saw a new industry and opportunity I never considered before. I didn't have to crawl on my hands and knees or be out in the heat, cold, rain, or snow and I could do more to contribute to a more productive society. I embraced the opportunity. Well sort of. For three years I was trying to do both because I was determined to build my own empire. The key lesson was, I was trying to do my own thing for me, not necessarily for the good of others. When Family Wealth started producing and selling its own products (i.e. books, online curriculum, audios, etc.) to people, organizations, churches and companies, it got really exciting.

—$ **TAKE BACK YOUR WEALTH!** $—

The cash accumulated inside the Wealth Legacy Plan is the equity or ownership interest inside the account which can be lent or leveraged for greater returns.

LIFETIME & LEGACY WEALTH

The Wealth Legacy Plan can be overlaid with bank financing from a business owner's financials alone or in addition to a person money paid into plan to get two to three times the benefits over a 25 to 40-year period of time. With more funding early on, the plan becomes a sizable bank for accessing money for a down payment on apartment units or business franchises or other major moves and use a portion of profits to pay back into plan. What is monumental is that it only takes a phone call to access after preliminary waiting period.

So for high income earners, entertainers, and athletes making $100K or more a year, if a 25 year old paid into plan as little as $200K as a lump sum (spread over first 5 years) coupled with approximately $600K of bank financing (over first ten years), by the time the person reaches their 60's, they can potentially have access to over $2.8M of tax free cash accumulated vs. $1.2M funding their plan solely by themselves. The tax-free lifetime income also potentially increases from $108K per year when self-funded to a projected $400K per year. This is a game changer! This is in addition to all of the other features including enhanced legacy (death) benefits, catastrophic illness benefits, downside protection, and more. Do I have your attention? The multi-layered Wealth Legacy Plan can be customized to any age and amount over age 18. Look at the possibilities in the below illustration based on the 25-year-old scenario.

Moving from **Lack** to *Abundance*

All licensed and non-licensed agents had to go through this process to be certified Family Wealth presenters and financial educators. That is why there are Wealth Ambassadors (those who are not licensed agents) and Wealth Strategists (those who are licensed agents with other professional occupations like a Realtor or accountant). We all were required to learn and apply information first hand to be an example of Five Star Success Living. That is why we are called Wealth Builders too. A speaker's bureau was formed and I found myself on the speakers circuit, motivating and inspiring people from various demographics as far as ethnic backgrounds, age ranges, income ranges, educational and professional designations at high schools, colleges, corporate functions, etc. Who would have thought a country boy from Sumter, SC, a city of only 40,000 people would be a national speaker for a wealth movement of the 21st century. I get excited just saying it.

I followed a financial game plan that was laid out for me five years ago regarding purchasing a duplex or fourplex. I bought the fourplex, before getting married, I stayed in one unit and had a roommate for the 2nd room in my unit and rented out the other three units. After about two years, I was paying two times the mortgage payment and by the third year, I had moved into my single-family home and was married shortly thereafter. I found out that women love when men got their financial house in order. Yes!!

For my residential home, it was a Subject To, meaning I paid the owner a lump sum to move on with their lives and sign over the home to me. I assumed the mortgage and interest in the property through a Quit Claim Deed. The property had equity in it, so I paid the equity value to the seller and they did not have to pay the traditional Realtor broker fees and seller fees. They saved and pocketed $5K more by doing our transaction. Fast forward, the fourplex is almost paid for and my current residence will be paid for free and clear in two more years.

SELF FUNDED VS BANK FUNDED

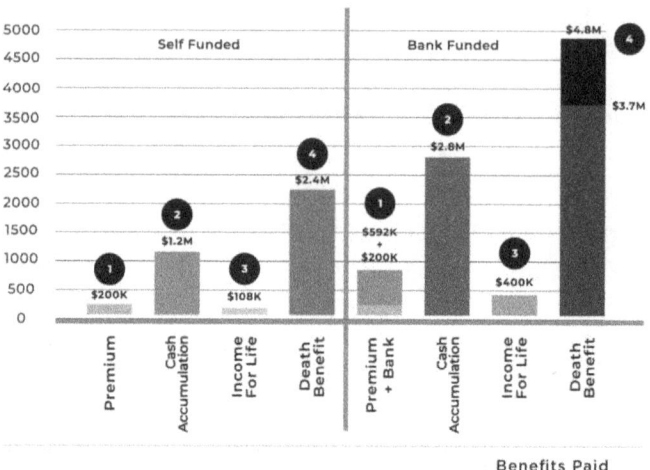

Benefits Paid At Age 60

Even with all of the lifetime wealth benefits, there are still legacy (death) benefits paid out after death, tax free. The idea is to front load the plan with $3 from bank funds for every $1 personally put in. Put more money on the front end or in early years so that on the back end or in latter years, there is more lifetime and legacy benefits and accessible cash to work with. The banking strategy is to leverage Wealth Legacy Plan, borrow from bank and build greater assets or benefits as a result.

Member of Family Wealth: Marques, you said a lot so far. You talked about how you started down one path with the HVAC business, got involved with Family Wealth and began to shift gears with financial services and speaking engagements. What do you say to the idea of staying down the path of mastery for 10,000 hours in seven to ten years?

Marques: I say, have a plan and move toward the goal or vision. Since we don't know it all and we make decisions based on our limited background, stay open to your hidden potential. Many people have left engineering or practicing law or accounting or even pastoring for that matter to do what we do. Because, I think deep down inside we all want to make a difference and impact the lives of others in our lifetime. It just feels like the right thing to do.

Member of Family Wealth: Marques, you mentioned acquiring a Subject To property. Why not just finance the property the traditional way?

Marques: Great question. Thanks for asking. I could have easily done the traditional financing; however, it was a deal that was not FOR SALE but ON SALE, meaning on discount. The owner had a dilemma of acquiring the home as an inheritance, not having the money to fix up the house to rent it out or sell it, so they just wanted the equity value and to be relieved of the house burden as fast as possible. I solved the owner's problem, picked up equity and a low existing interest rate of 3.2%. I found great handymen and contractors over the years so fixing up the place took me less than three months.

—$ **TAKE BACK YOUR WEALTH!** $—

Questions For Review & Reflection:

1) How would you classify your organization based on the five listed?

2) Could your organization benefit from your supporters having access to an online curriculum offered on your website?

3) What would achieving Five Star Success mean to you?

4) What difference would it make to have children practice the financial principles and practices early in life?

5) How can the Wealth Legacy Plan help you buy and build lifetime & legacy wealth?

— Moving from **Lack** to *Abundance* —

Visitor of Family Wealth: This community is off the charts when it comes to information, tools, and strategies. My head is spinning. Everything sounds new!

Kimbell: Unfortunately, it is. We all thought and felt the same way when we were first introduced to all of this information. After a while, it became second nature and once you master the Five Star Success money skill sets, you just duplicate and multiply. This is why many of us are trending millionaires today.

Visitor of Family Wealth: Millionaires plural?

Kimbell: Yes. You heard right. Five Star Success is the blueprint to not only achieving the base level of skill sets but building upon the foundation to ultimately become financially free. Once financially free, then the next destination is to become a millionaire in your lifetime and make millionaire children in their lifetime and create generational wealth forever! And what's so beautiful about it is, this is the way it was supposed to be from the very beginning. Finally, Tony Robbins said, *"If you want to build wealth, get in front of a trend,"* that is what Nicole and I did five years ago and continue doing today.

Visitor of Family Wealth: Sign Me Up Today!!

Shaughn Lee: I know you are excited. I was too when I first start hearing and applying this information. Tani is one of our early members also and have been meeting with her adult children for years. Care to share your testimony Tani?

ially.
CHAPTER # FIVE

POSTERITY OF FIVE STAR SUCCESS

Moving from **Lack** to *Abundance*

FAMILY WEALTH COMMUNITY
ENGAGEMENT OF CONCEPTS
- Continued -

TRANSFORM TO GREATER FOR PRESERVATION

Achieving Five Star Success and using the various principles and rules of money and wealth ushers in a whole new level of living. Having a different mindset paradigm begins to transition you from a consumer to creator, from debtor to lender (or owner) and from laborer to wealth builder.

It is desired that you not only master the five-money skill sets within ten years, but prosper greatly as you teach and demonstrate a champion lifestyle to your spouse or significant other and your children and children's children. Like the Rothschilds and Rockefellers, abundance must be turned into lifetime and legacy wealth.

As you have seen, it is not a matter of how much you earn, but rather what can be created, preserved, grown, and transferred to later years and beyond for posterity sake.

Please keep in mind that our money system has no intrinsic value. It is created out of thin air and only has the value based on the belief that it can be used for trade and commerce. It is advised that it is not stored in its original state because it does not have any lasting or inherit value. It is easily devalued by inflation. Like the board game Monopoly indicated in the rules of the game, buy assets (buy properties or staple industries as fast as possible). In other words, convert cash into an equivalent product or service that can increase or store value for longer periods of time. The conversion can be in investments or businesses. There can be buying, selling, being sued and suing under business entities or investment groups.

PROTECT & PRESERVE ASSETS FOREVER

Think of you and your family as a professional baseball team playing

FAMILY BUSINESS & TRUST AFFAIRS

Tani: Sure, thanks Shaughn Lee. It is really amazing when having a strategic plan and being held accountable to walk out the plan, how much can be accomplished. Like yourself, I set up a Trust to preserve my estate but wanted my children to be aware and very savvy in carrying on what I built. So around four years ago, in addition to our mother, children dates, I started having family meetings at least once a month. In our meetings, we had a template for a corporation or organization key roles. We have the CEO or President, the COO or Vice-President, the CFO or Treasurer and CIO or Secretary. I started as the President of our family wealth meetings. My eldest son was and is the Vice President and next in line to run the family's affairs. He is a Durable Power of Attorney to handle both financial and health decisions if I become incapacitated. Upon my demise, he steps into the role of Trustee and Executor of the Estate. My wishes are inside the Will which are placed inside the Trust. My second eldest is in the military. He lives out of state however he still participates in the family meetings as the Treasurer, pulling off monthly reports as it pertains to my rental income for the home, the family owned fast food franchises and Mary Kay business. My brother acts as the Assistant Treasurer. My daughter acts as the recording Secretary with my youngest son being the Assistant Secretary in her absence. We have a corporate binder and a Trust binder that we keep the notes (or minutes) in along with banking reports, tax filings, and other pertinent information as it pertains to the family businesses and the Trust respectively. We use the Roberts Rules of Order for calling meeting to order, voting, tabling discussion items and bringing meeting to a close. I am fortunate to see how my affairs will be ran without me regarding my personal finances, the family businesses and the Trust. I feel very

against a formidable opponent who have taken out many people and business owners. Your opponent strikeout teams most of the time with a 95% winning streak. People and business owners oftentimes end up broke, busted, disgusted, and working for the rest of their lives. Furthermore, all that is left to pass on to the next generation is debt vs. wealth, meaning a losing record is passed on from generation to generation. The formidable opponents are D.I.R.T (Debt, Inflation, Retirement Vehicles, and Taxes). There are the Five Money Systems also seeking to leverage you and your family's time, energy and resources through Credit, Cash Flow, Business, Banking, and Investments. The nine players all have their roles on the field to prevent you and your family from running the bases and scoring home runs.

Through Five Star Success training, you learn how to navigate your finances and businesses to progress from base to base with the strategy to Leverage, Borrow, and Build Assets. You learn how to buy into or build business systems to get on home plate to get up to bat. You don't settle for riding the bench, working the '9-5 job' for extended periods of time. You launch the business perhaps with a single hit, double or triple hit. Maybe there are some setbacks like getting striked out and you have to change partners or products or services, but you set out to grow and expand your business to get some runs to home base. With those victories, the business acquires some assets to get on the scoreboard for passive income, safe and lasting wealth. Making assets acquired by a family business safe and available for use for generations is called a Trust. Look at the baseball diamond visual and how you can win more than you lose, how you can gain more surplus vs. lack.

confident, that what I have started can continue until infinity. Let me say that each family should ascertain if they have children or relatives that they can trust, if not then you may want to look at business partners, accountants, law firms, or other trusted advisors to carry out roles of Trustee or Executor of Estate. What I have established for my family may not be conducive for others.

Member of Family Wealth: I heard how some families conduct affairs at family reunions, but I haven't heard of conducting affairs within the family in that manner. How young were your children when you started having these meetings?

Tani: Great question. All I can say is start with your children as soon as they know what is going on. I'll say around seven or eight years old. My children were adults when we started having meetings because I didn't know about this stuff.

Shaughn Lee: Thank you so much Tani. Setting up Wills and Trusts are so wise and valuable to the family. It avoids a whole lot of chaos, confusion, and hurt feelings. When establishing them early, like Tani, each of us can see if any adjustments need to be made along the way before death to ensure the estate lives on. Excellent! I want to turn our attention to a gentleman who facilitated these meetings when I joined Family Wealth. He and his wife visit with us every now and then and we are so grateful for their presence this evening. I must ask them to come up and share some words of their journey from lack to abundance. Help me welcome Pastor Sean and Lady Kim. (Everyone applauds)

—$ **TAKE BACK YOUR WEALTH!** $—

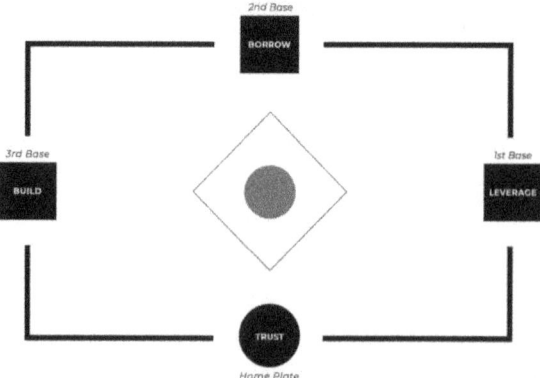

Ideally, businesses are for back and forth transactions like running from base to base. However, when it is time to preserve assets for safekeeping, they need to be placed inside of a Trust (ran into home base).

In the book, What Would The Rockefellers Do, there were two powerful instruments used by the Rockefeller family to safeguard wealth and ensure it lasted for generations. The two financial instruments were cash value insurance and a Trust. Since we touched on cash value insurance in previous chapters, let's focus on a Trust and elements of estate planning.

A Trust is a legal entity created to control the distribution of property or management of income producing assets. It is entrusting valuable items of the owner into another's care for preservation and safekeeping. The formal definition is granting a person or entity the fiduciary responsibility of holding the title to property or assets for the benefit of another. Therefore, there is the:

Grantor who is the person or entity desiring the Trust to be formed between themselves and another, who will *"fund"* the trust in his or her lifetime.

Moving from **Lack** to *Abundance*

LAW of the LID

Pastor Sean: Thank you Shaughn Lee for the opportunity. We are honored to be visiting with you this evening. It is truly a blessing to see how an idea and commitment can manifest miracles. Amen. All of us are miracles as we have transformed from lack to abundance, from a place of economic bondage to financial freedom. It is true what John Maxwell says about the Law of the Lid, meaning any organization, family, or company can only rise as far as the leadership of the entity or group. Lady Kim and I had to really face some tough decisions about five years ago because we had a growing church, a construction company, a home, two children in college, one child still at home, two luxury cars and from the outside looking in, it looked like we were the Family of the Year. Amen.

We thought we had arrived ourselves and living the American Dream, not fully understanding how fake we were and what negative impact we were having on our congregation members. They reflected the façade of designer clothes, nice cars, living in nice homes and popular neighborhoods. Everyone looked wonderful and were proud of our newly built church building. Everyone loved paying their kingdom building offerings in addition to their tithes and offerings. Our viewpoint changed when we were convicted by seeing all of the money raised from widows, people on fixed incomes, and struggling congregation members bring hard earned money to the church for the church to simply give a big chunk to the banks for our large mortgage on the building. The people did not own anything and furthermore did not have insurance to bury loved ones nor Wills or Trusts in place. When people would die, there was so much drama and family members would leave the church or fall out with each other over he said, she said arguments. Church members were setting up Go Fund Me accounts or we were taking up special collections for the family to bury loved ones. Oftentimes houses were foreclosed on and cars repossessed because there were mortgages

—$ TAKE BACK YOUR 𝓦EALTH! $—

Trustee is the caretaker or manager of the entrusted estate and assets given certain instructions, duties, powers and discretion to manage the Trust on behalf of the heirs of the estate.

A beneficiary is the person or entity who benefits from the perpetual estate. Benefits can include shelter, driving certain cars, certain allowances, having certain education expenses paid for, marriage costs, business startup funding, unemployment benefits, down payment or purchase of own home, graduation presents, hospital payments, etc.

A Trust has a separation of Legal Title and Equity Title. The Legal Title is held by the Trustee which is 'Apparent Ownership' or a person or entity with controlling or managing interest in the property, business, or investment. The Equity Title is having use or privilege of the assets provided which are spelled out in the Trust for the benefit of heirs or stated beneficiaries. Note: A beneficiary could be a charitable organization also.

The Trust is a powerful contractual agreement that can do several things for the protecting and preserving of the estate.

1) The Trust can provide Asset Protection from liens, judgments, and lawsuits because legally the assets have been transferred out of your possession to the possession of another (or the Trust). You no longer carry the Legal Title. Nelson Rockefeller said, *"Own nothing, control everything."*

2) The Trust can provide Privacy whereas it is not public information. It can only be viewed and accessed by the entrusted party, therefore the Trustee.

3) The Trust is not subject to probate, therefore the transfer of assets are not subject to probate fees, nor can the distribution of property get tied up in state courts.

4) The Trust can reduce inheritance and estate taxes above the exemptions, when other Trusts, Foundations, or Endowments are set up due to assets not being transferred to heirs but enjoyed by them and the estate continuing as if the original Grantor were still alive. This is the idea around 'Living Forever.'

and car notes still outstanding on people in their 60's and 70's.

On top of all that Lady Kim and I were riddled with expenses and debt ourselves, living paycheck to paycheck feeling a little anxious about our future as we were getting older. Amen. (Pastor Sean glances at Lady Kim and she speaks)

Lady Kim: I remember when Sean and I sat down with "General" and he asked us some hard questions about four areas of our spending. They were regarding the cable bill, the cell phone bill, the luxury cars, and the dining out. This was on top of having two children in college and one still at home. We found out how much money we were wasting, and I'll never forget how we submitted to the advice and freed up $2,300 a month in 30 days. From that point we were determined to get a handle on our personal finances and learn more effective strategies to secure our financial future, so we may teach others.

We saw how pertinent it was to include practical application of God's word. We had to answer the questions, *"How do we exercise the power to gain wealth...How do we become the lender and not the borrower...How do we cancel all debt with our neighbor and...How do we leave an inheritance for our children's children?"* Once we got clear answers and understood how to accomplish these things, we began to preach it and teach it. We did not just talk about tithes and offerings, but we talked about paying yourself first at least 10 percent for building long-term wealth. We talked about delayed gratification and paying as you go, saving for emergency fund and future purchases, to not carry debt.

We set up the Five Star Success standards in our church and began to have people share testimonies about their accomplishments. Some would share how they created more passive income to have more time freedom. Others would give praise reports around achieving 700+ credit scores, because the Bible says that a good name is to be desired more than silver and gold. We taught that credit was not for debt purposes but for leverage purposes. It is what was meant by

—$ TAKE BACK YOUR *W*EALTH! $—

All Trusts are not created equal. How they are structured and worded establishes the strength, the perpetuity, and the jurisdiction of the Trust. Going into the details of Trusts are beyond the scope of this book, however there are some basics to be aware of. A Living Trust is very common, where the decision to transfer assets to and from the Trust is revocable. This means the Grantor can change his or her mind. It becomes irrevocable after the Grantor dies. This is also known as a Grantor's Trust. It provides privacy but not much asset protection during the Grantor's lifetime.

Another structure of a Trust is one that is irrevocable where the assets are transferred to the Trust irrevocably, meaning the Grantor cannot change their mind and transfer assets out of the Trust at will. The assets are managed from the Trustee going forward. This type of Trust carries more asset protection during a Grantor's lifetime.

There are levels of Trusts which are statutory, therefore governed by and under the jurisdiction of the United States. Thus, there was an old legal principle called the *rule against perpetuities* used to prohibit trusts that could potentially last forever. Oversimplified, it stated that a Trust couldn't last more than 21 years after the death of a potential beneficiary who was alive when the Trust was created. Some states have adopted the Uniform Statutory Rule Against Perpetuities which allows a Trust to last about 90 years. There is also a non-statutory Trust otherwise known as a Common Law or Pure Trust. *"A Pure Trust is not subject to legislative control..."* Croker v. MacCloy, 649 US Supp 39. In essence, a Trust set up properly under the proper jurisdiction can cause an estate to last forever.

A strategy used by the Rockefellers and other rich and wealthy families have the Trust own cash value insurance policies, have the death benefit on the insured, meaning yourself, a member of the family, or heir and the beneficiary of the insurance policy be the Trust also. Please note that an individual, business entity, or Trust can both own and be the beneficiary of policies as long as there is an insurable interest at the time of application.

When you or a family member or heir dies, instead of the death benefit going directly to a named beneficiary or heir, the proceeds go to the Trust.

Moving from Lack to *Abundance*

walking circumspectly in the world. We encouraged everyone to buy and own their home and rid all debt in ten years or less and to have an ownership position in cash value insurance, businesses, stocks, bonds, gold, and silver.

We set up a Wealth Building Center in our church and began to help other churches around the country set up similar centers with certified financial education instructors. The WBC's help people learn about financial principles, money rules, and wealth rules. Furthermore, we worked with Family Wealth to launch the online curriculum so as an overall community, we may connect with social organizations, financial institutions, charitable organizations, and more to change the financial landscape for millions of Americans. Our objective was and is to lead the masses toward Five Star Success as a base of money skill sets to duplicate practices and multiply wealth.

We spread our unique message of wealth building and prosperity via live streaming and the people began gravitating toward the truth. It is indeed setting the people free from debt, from working 30 plus years on a job, from leaving debt vs. wealth and being stressed and concerned about making ends meet. It is a new day for us and for the thousands we get to touch through the practical application of God's word. We have calls and praise reports pouring in all over America about how people are accomplishing so much more financially. I am talking about doctors, lawyers, engineers, nurses, other pastors, professors and teachers, firefighters, police officers, artists, sports stars, etc. The list goes on and on. As a result, tithes and offerings are pouring in at a rate we never could imagine. Since making the online curriculum accessible to the supporters of various organizations, charities are getting a boost in giving, social organizations get more participation, financial institutions help more people start businesses and educational institutions add more financial education into their curriculum as well.

Pastor Sean: This is the Lord's doing and it is truly marvelous in our eyes. Amen. We are experiencing a modern-day Exodus moving the people from bondage to

—$ TAKE BACK YOUR *Wealth!* $—

The Trustee takes the lump sum and purchases paid up insurance policies on the children, grandchildren, and great grandchildren and the remaining amounts are paid out based on life events such as marriage, unemployment periods, starting a business, going to college, being hospitalized, buying a car, etc. Other funds or income gets invested conservatively into other investments to build greater assets and grow estate's portfolio.

There are comprehensive Trusts made where the timeline can be for 100 + years outlining today's payout amounts and increasing based on an inflation average being, let's say 3% each year. The frequency is set also, meaning for a car, it may be $30K in today's dollars and the next payout may be in ten years for $39K based on 130% (ten years x 3% inflation). Let's have some fun with these scenarios and show how you too can literally operate like Mayer Amschel Rothschild and set up a dynasty to last forever where your children, children's children and beyond will have their basic needs met. The good book says, *"A Good Man (Or Woman) Leaves An Inheritance For His Children's Children."*

Without getting too complicated, let's examine the below scenario as if it took effect when the grandchildren were adults. If having four grandchildren, and all benefits were used by all four grandchildren over a 30-year period of time, that would be roughly $2.4M used vs. $4.0M grown in one asset. If there were eight great grandchildren and they used all benefits over another 30 years, that would be roughly another $8M used. The combined totals for the grands and great grands would be roughly $10.5M vs. $32M accumulated over a 60-year time period. Over a 100-year period, one asset starting at $500K (death benefit) could grow inside a 7% vehicle and double every ten years to accumulate $10.27B for your estate. Hi Mr. and Mrs. Rothschild imitators!

freedom. Because most of the leaders in our church are financially independent, we don't take a salary therefore our tithes and offerings are being poured back into the community and our congregation members lives through a Community Trust Fund. It is revolutionary! It will help the people achieve Five Star Success even faster.

Visitor of Family Wealth: Whoa! What are you saying Pastor Sean? I never heard of that before. What are you saying?

Pastor Sean: (Pastor Sean smiles) Let's just say I am being prophetic at this time for the vision is for an appointed time. Amen.

Visitor of Family Wealth: It sounds like you and Lady Kim are pretty progressive and what you are doing sounds like a fresh approach to bringing resolution to what has been ailing the people, even myself for that matter.

Pastor Sean: We think so too. People are tired of church as usual and want to see their lives more fulfilled with less stress. We were encouraged to repent from our error, our pride and ego feeding to turn toward the principles and precepts that were tried and true and turn toward meeting the needs of the people. There is a proper order to everything, something comes first, then second, then third, etc. Without order, there is chaos and without a vision, the people perish. Seek wisdom, it is the principal thing and in all your getting of information, gain understanding. Those words are as true today as they were when they were first written. We have been living in abundance ever since we corrected the error of our ways and we encourage everyone in the room to sincerely consider all that have been shared with you today if you really want to turn your finances around.

—$ **TAKE BACK YOUR 𝓦EALTH!** $—

LIFE EVENT	PAY OUT AMOUNTS	FREQUENCY	YEAR 10	YEAR 50	YEAR 100
Marriage	Up to $20K	Once In A Lifetime	Up to $26K	Up to $50K	Up to $80K
Car	Up to $30K	Every 10 Years Up To 3 Times	Up to $39K	Up to $75K	Up to $120K
Down Payment On House	Up to $50K	Every 10 Years Up To 3 Times	Up to $65K	Up to $125K	Up to $200K
Education	Up to $30K	Up To 2 times In 10 Years	Up to $39K	Up to $75K	Up to $120K
Unemployment	Up to $1.5K	Up To 18 Months	Up to $1.95K	Up to $3.75K	Up to $6.0K
Starting A Business	Up to $50K	Every 10 Years Up To 3 Times	Up to $65K	Up to $125K	Up to $200K
Death & Burial	Up to $10K	Once In A Lifetime	Up to $13K	Up to $25K	Up to $40K
TRUST ASSET	$500K	Double Every 10 Years	$1.0M	$16M	$10.27B

The purpose of paying out during life events and during intervals is based on Preserving The Principal and Minimizing The Distributions, that means allow the capital asset to grow as long as possible while minimizing the distributions to the heirs. Using this perpetual strategy, money can be made available for the life needs of all heirs for an infinite number of generations to come.

The same concept works for major institutions like the Harvard Endowment Fund. Harvard was founded in Cambridge, Massachusetts in 1636. Harvard University endowment fund was valued at $37.6B as of 2015. The Endowment distributed $1.8B in fiscal year ending June 30, 2017. An Endowment is made by a Foundation for the purposes of planned systematic withdrawal for its sole purpose and the remaining (the principal) continues to grow for succeeding generations of students, staff, research, upkeep of facilities, etc.

Wills can accompany a Trust regarding the disposition of furniture heirlooms, cars, etc. The Last Will & Testament is a list of last wishes or desires of the departed regarding his or her intimate items and the

— Moving from Lack to *Abundance* —

Shaughn Lee: Wow, that was powerful Pastor Sean. Any final remarks Lady Kim?

Lady Kim: Follow principles and precepts instead of trends and fads. Be connected to like-minded people moving in your desired direction. Among such people you will find inspiration, instruction and support and accountability along the way. As Zig Ziglar said, may he rest in peace, *"You can have anything in life, if you help enough people get what they want."* This is now what we live by. When you get surplus, know what to do with it, so you may convert it to lifetime and legacy wealth.

Shaughn Lee: That is a great word, I feel like we should be passing the offering plate around. (Everyone laughs)

TIME & PROGRESS

After 20 years, Family Wealth still meets, and numerous communities, organizations, and churches have followed the Five Star Success Living concepts. Each generation is being taught by the succeeding generation. Families are having discussions about money, their business, and the affairs of their estate. Family Trusts also own business systems, stocks and bonds, gold and silver, residential and commercial real estate and are managed by financially savvy Trustees to minimize debt service and maximize returns without breaking the rules for building wealth.

affairs of the estate. If placed inside the Trust, there will be privacy and the Trustee will seek to carry out the requests accordingly.

If there is no Trust, then at the very least, there should be a Will with an assigned Executor of The Estate to handle funeral arrangements and expenses, probating the Will and carrying out disposition of items to avoid chaos, disagreements and hurt feelings.

The Trustee or Executor of The Estate may be the same or different persons or entities. Both should be capable of handling the short term and long-term financial affairs of the estate.

A way to prepare Trustees or people to step up to run different aspects of the family business or heritage is to have family meetings once or twice a month. There is the corporate reference or organization reference point of assigning at least four roles.

    1) CEO or President

    2) COO or Vice President

    3) CIO or Secretary

    4) CFO or Treasurer

The roles or titles can be given whether there is a family business or not. The household should run affairs as a structured and organized unit. Only decide if role references are corporate or organization centered. The meetings can be among immediate family members, i.e. husband, wife, children or among adult family members who are cousins, uncles, aunts, grandchildren, etc. Whoever the group is, there must be cohesiveness and a spirit of unity and agreement.

Moving from Lack to *Abundance*

Let's catch up with the Family Wealth Community 20 years after the concept was initiated.

Marques: Welcome to our special anniversary event this evening to honor the work of a group of people who changed the financial landscape for millions of Americans. I am now in my 50's and living life on my own terms. I have been doing so for about 15 years. It is so amazing to me! So far, I have lived far above my wildest dreams. Who would have ever imagined me becoming a millionaire in my lifetime, not to mention within ten years. I was in my early 30's when I started with Family Wealth. I think that says a lot about being at the forefront of a major wealth movement like ours, you can't help but reap tremendous benefits when helping so many people go from lack to abundance. We also made many millionaires over the years and they are making millionaires of their children and children's children.

Because of the information obtained and support of the community, not only did I change my paradigm around money's purpose, but I commanded money to work harder for me than I worked for it. And so did many others. We created a culture where the 20 and 30-year-olds would use corporate jobs and income to fund their passion and purpose and would take all ten years to perfect their craft, their inventions or services for the marketplace (outside the workplace). They would package up and distribute their value proposition to the market in exchange for their reward. If they loved their occupations or careers, they definitely would put money into the most effective vehicles for building lifetime and legacy wealth.

Tonight, we wanted to pay honor to some of the pioneers who had such a vision

—$ TAKE BACK YOUR *WEALTH!* $—

As CEO or President, this is often the head of household responsible for generating income and accumulating capital for the household, company, or organization. This person strategizes, envisions, and gives direction to the organized body.

As COO or Vice President, this is often the spouse or most responsible child who ensures that the operations of the household (or organization) are ran in a smooth manner on a day to day basis. This person is second in command.

As CFO or Treasurer, this person can be a spouse or child who manages the joint banking accounts of the household (or business) ensuring money is in place to cover payables, i.e. expenses, debt payments, taxes, savings and investments. This person reports on income vs. expenses and asset values vs. liabilities to determine discretionary income and net worth. Go to **worksheet.familywealthtoday.com** to fill out form for personal or business purposes.

As CIO or Secretary, this person can be a spouse or child who documents the minutes of the family (or business meetings). The correspondence is kept in cloud storage, on USB drive or in family (or corporate) binder using acid free paper.

It is imperative that the family or business have trusted advisors for which to draw information, techniques and strategies from. The family or corporate structure could look like the diagram to the right.

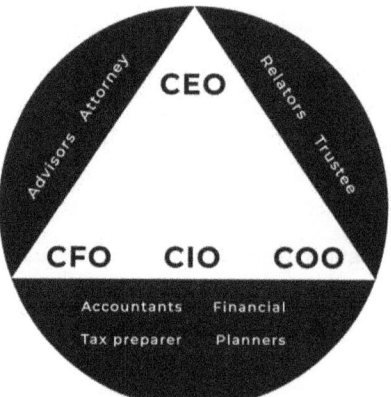

Moving from Lack to *Abundance*

from the beginning and walked the vision out day in and day out, week in and week out, year in and year out to what it is today. Help me welcome to the stage Shaughn Lee and Aviance. (Everyone applauds)

Shaughn Lee and Aviance: Thank you so much. (Shaughn Lee looks at Aviance) Baby, we did it and we are doing it.

Aviance: I am so grateful to be here tonight and to have walked out this amazing journey. For us to do in one generation what many thought would take over 100 years to accomplish is a miracle in itself. It goes to show the power of unity and agreement and how it can speed up processes and attract more resources.

Shaughn Lee: You are so right, "General" would tell us, that unity would be the secret to our success. Unity in the home and unity in the community. What we thought was almost impossible to do as far as getting people on one accord and moving toward a common cause somehow became possible. The people were ready for change, ready for more passion, more purpose, a greater quality of life, and making a bigger impact on society. So once our first Family Wealth book came out in year one, then our online curriculum the next year along with our connecting with various organizations across the country, the information in regards to changing mindsets quickly spread. People, families, and communities began to come together and move together toward Five Star Success. It was tangible. People could check their achievements which were actual money skill sets off the list and build upon their successes.

We created these lapel pins to denote those who have completed the Five Star Success process. We call them Master Champions, those who have mastered the basics of personal finance. Then we created the next level curriculum and criteria to reach Master Champion II and III. You will notice that all of us so called pioneers have reached the higher levels as well, it is because after the mastery of the basics, there is only duplication and multiplication required to become very wealthy.

—$ **TAKE BACK YOUR WEALTH!** $—

There is not enough time in a day to become efficient in all areas alone, so trusted advisors help family to obtain the key information or services needed to make quicker, calculated risk decisions.

Having these kinds of family (or business) meetings in addition to having trusted advisors ensures that all is informed about the family affairs and any person can step up and into the vacant role at any time.

In summary, wealth is transferred through insurance and other investment vehicles and a Trust manages assets to protect and preserve assets through smaller distributions over specified periods of time. Money wisdom is passed along with organized family (or business) practices for generations to pass down to cancel more debt and lack and present a life of ample supply. Use Robert Rules Of Order Handbook.

THE CONCLUSIVE SUMMARY

Thank you for your time and attention while reading through this book. There was much shared from principles, rules, tools, skills, standards, and strategies to help you go from lack to abundance. As with a Rubik's cube which was baffling to most and easy for a few to solve back in the 1980s...

The **Code Breaker Of Lack To Abundance** is simply five things and they are:

1) Own And Build Business Systems to create passive, residual income streams to replace earned income in a lifetime.

2) Market To The Masses by packaging and distributing gifts and talents for the greater good of mankind.

3) Leverage, Borrow & Build Assets by leveraging ideas, credit, cash flow or collateral to borrow from others, banks or own banking systems to acquire more things of lasting and intrinsic value.

We said from the beginning, if you can master $24K in passive income, you can...

Members of Family Wealth: Master $48K!

Shaughn Lee: And if you can master $48K, you can...

Members of Family Wealth: Master $96K!

Shaughn Lee: For the name of the game is to...

Members of Family Wealth: Replace earned income!

Shaughn Lee: And when you have replaced earned income, you are...

Members of Family Wealth: Financially Free! (Everyone yells and applauds)

Aviance: The larger our community or network got, the more endorsements, sponsors and grants we received. It was as though all were waiting in a long line for Family Wealth to arrive. We arrived and are growing leaps and bounds thanks to all of you. It is your dedication and commitment that will carry this legacy on for several decades. You are awesome! Thanks Marques for the platform.

Marques: Wow! That was great. Thank you two for all you have done regarding this Family Wealth Movement. Next, I want to bring up the super power couple, Kimbell and Nicole. All of us mere mortals call Kimbell, Kimbellman.

Kimbell: (Kimbell laughs) Boy, it is not easy being a superhero, I get picked on and laughed at but someone has to do it. (Kimbell looks at crowd and smiles). What can I say, this has been phenomenal. Nicole and I recall desiring a change of pace which precipitated our move from Austin, Texas to Charlotte, NC. I landed my job in my field, then I met Shaughn Lee, then the "General" and we began to forge ahead to building out the Family Wealth Community and Movement.

My son was only three years old when I joined forces with the community and he is 23 years old today. He has already made a half a million dollars a year at his age, most of it passively. He never had to work for anyone else. We brought him up in our businesses of real estate, insurance, and some inventions and he

—$ TAKE BACK YOUR *WEALTH!* $—

4) Secure Base With Wealth Legacy Plan so there is a fundamental and foundational financial instrument that will build wealth automatically. Other financial vehicles can be layered on top of it.

5) Transfer & Preserve Wealth With A Trust is a way to carry wealth forward for generations to benefit from and follow suit by adding more assets and Trusts over their lifetime as well. It will create a snowball effect of enormous estate wealth like the very rich and wealthy around the world.

We have come full circle with the code breaker to imitate the Three in One System based on cash flow, leverage, and equity. To create cash flow we own and build business systems and market to the masses. For leverage, we use banking strategies to leverage, borrow, and build assets. For equity, Wealth Legacy Plans build cash value and Trusts preserve assets for perpetual management and growth.

We at Family Wealth truly hope you have gained some nuggets of wisdom to help you live a life at Five Star Success Levels. This is our earnest desire for you.

Join the Wealth Movement! Take back your wealth now and forever. We are looking for Chapters to be formed around the country to help build wealth building communities. You can help up to four ways:

1) Become a Wealth Ambassador (Promote & Attend Events)

2) Become a Wealth Strategist (Become a Licensed Professional)

3) Become a Wealth Builder (Be a Customer & Example)

4) Become a Business Strategist (Help Other Businesses Grow)

For more information, contact us at Family Wealth, *"Strategies For Financial Success."*

— Moving from Lack to *Abundance* —

has been able to improve upon and expand what we have built.

Nicole: That's right. And what we did for our children, is what I only imagined. I remembered how Donald Trump who was President of the United States 20 years ago, had three older children who stepped in and ran his Trump brand empire and how they were worth at least $150M each while their father was a billionaire. It can be done by us for our children too. We just have to do the work ourselves to get the empire started.

Marques: Thank you so much Kimbell and Nicole for your words of wisdom. It is my pleasure to introduce a gentleman who we affectionately call the General who envisioned all that we accomplished coming to present. Help me welcome the "General" (the audience applauds).

"GENERAL:" Thank you so much Marques for carrying the Family Wealth vision forward to the next generation. I am also grateful for all of the pioneers who have come before me to be able to build upon. What a phenomenal celebration we have. One of the key things I want to express this evening as it pertains to wealth building is to focus on passive income. It took me eight years to crack the code as it pertains to owning and building a business system and marketing to the masses. Once one system could generate $2K per month, then results could be leveraged, money reinvested into Social Media, marketing, product and service enhancements to raise (borrow) more funds through equity shares or short-term loans (one to three years). This is how I was able to build the system and systems to scale. Mastering these three steps is what multiplied passive income for me and snowballed Five Star Success.

Remember this very important truth, with more income, 700+ credit scores can easily be maintained for personal rewards, real estate can be acquired and owned free and clear, all debt cancelled very quickly with other investments made and businesses created for building enormous equity in assets. And once acquiring your five layers of financial portfolio (insurance, gold and silver, real estate, stocks

—$ **TAKE BACK YOUR WEALTH!** $—

Questions For Review & Reflection:

1) How many businesses do you have set up for tax advantages and asset protection?

2) Do you have a Will and Family Trust set up? Will you choose to set both up in the near future?

3) What life events would you include when setting up a Trust for multiple generations?

4) How can you imitate the Three in One System for cash flow, leverage, and equity?

5) What role of the four do you see yourself playing to help further our wealth empowerment initiative?

and bonds and businesses) simply protect them in the Trust to forward wealth to cancel lack and debt for generations to come.

It is my greatest pleasure to have helped millions see the light and several in this room to have reached multi-millionaire status by being early adopters of the concepts shared. My life is full and my purpose fulfilled. I honor you this evening for inspiring all the people we serve. Cheers to all of us for our contributions to our modern-day Exodus from lack to abundance (everyone raises their glasses, salutes, and cheers).

We fast forward to the end of the night after the audience heard from Tani, Demond, Ms. Darla, and Pastor Sean also. We join Marques as he concludes.

Marques: We certainly want to thank you all for coming out tonight. We have heard from the pioneers and we have taken the mantle and we continue to run with it. For any visitors in the room or if you have come out to our weekly events, you may hear us talk about Wealth Legacy Plans, and you may ask, "What is it exactly? What is a Wealth Legacy Plan?"…(He pauses, the members of Family Wealth smile)…Stay tuned. Get with a Wealth Strategist to show you how it can secure your financial future and jumpstart your children's financial future. Remember this statement, in honor of our great friend Marlon Smith…

"A vision without action is merely a dream. Action without vision just passes time but vision with action can change the world!"

Thanks for coming out. (The audience applauds)

ACKNOWLEDGEMENTS

This is recognition and thanks for all who have assisted me down this path of Financial Literacy and Empowerment since 2010. It is because of lending your time, talent, and treasure that I have been able to continue on this journey. There have been some twists and turns along the way, but the mission and vision remains the same, which are:

Mission: To Change Mindsets, To Build Businesses And Assets and Leave Worthwhile Legacies.

Vision: To Change The Financial Landscape For Millions Of Americans.

Thank you universe for all of the resources you have provided throughout the years for truly I am a witness of 'Provision For Vision.' I call my trek the miracle mile.

This list for recognition is like the credits to a blockbuster movie, listed in chronological order.

[From 2010—2011] Thank you: Sharise Lloyd, Ben & Keturah June, Jamar Matthews, Dethra Young, Hasan Harnett, Shari Hill, Attorney Eric Matthews, Attorney Paul Pedigo, Stoney Sellers, Mr. Duane Hill and Sean Langston.

[From 2013—2015] Thank you: Willie Crite Jr, Kenyon Graham, Oscar & Kiya Frazier, Johnesta Woods, Jack Brayboy, Dameon Workman, Saran Almond, Greg Wigfall, Dan Mallard, Charles Thomas, Roy Schoolfield, Yaminah Yisrael, Melissa Carter, Robin Blacknell, Daryl Briggs, Sarah Singletary, Mike Askew, Jasmine Wright, Rob 'B Smoov' Brown (RIP), Joan Bean, Larris Renner, Sudev Rajah, Kevin Battle, Vicky Foster and Crystal Callahan.

[From 2016—Present] Thank you: Tony Jackson, Marlon Smith, Dr. George C. Fraser, Black Wealth Alliance, Marlo Brayboy, Nicole Simpson, Pastor Damiko Faulkner, Catrese Kilgore and Carisa Hill, Leadership of First Financial Security, Family Wealth Community: Shaughn Lee, Kimbell Collins, Demond Raybon, Tashmonique Beverly, Chris Williams, Daryl Williams, Darryl Douglas, Gurmay Fraser, Eugene & Deborah Hash, Trenton Bullock, Pastor Sean Weaver, Altheia Anthony and others.

Thanks to Jonsehn Creative Group, our publisher for your time and dedication for assisting in bringing this book to market.

Thanks to my family members, Caleb Archer my only child for your patience with me and the sacrifices I have had to make to make a difference in the world we live in. Thank you very much mom, Ms. Carrie Merl Agee for always being the cheerleader of my aspirations. I love you mom. May you rest in peace. Thanks to Damon Williams who has been like a brother to me over 40 years and Sonia Staton, the sister I never knew growing up but am grateful for the close relationship we have now as well as my nieces Mikaela and Aliyah Staton and nephew Hugh Mari Cole.

To all contributors and supporters, your confidence in me, and the work I am called to do won't go unrewarded. Thanks again.

Sincerely,

Rodney D. Archer

For more information about the
Wealth Legacy Plans, go to:
wlp.familywealthtoday.com
For a FREE 25 minute consultation with a Wealth Strategist about setting up Wealth Legacy Plans and other financial strategies, call us at:
1-800-859-8455 ext. 101
or email us at:
info@familywealthtoday.com

To request a National Speaker from our
Family Wealth Community, call:
1-800-859-8455 ext. 102
or email us at:
speakers@familywealthtoday.com

Desiring to start a Family Wealth Community in your city or state? call:
1-800-859-8455 ext. 103
or email us at:
community@familywealthtoday.com

RESOURCES

PAGE #	SUBJECT OR QUOTE	SOURCE	NOTE
	About Rexnord Corps Relocation	Www.theindychannel.com 11/22/2017	Headline: Rexnord closes its Indy Plant for good.
	Retail Store Closings	Google: USA Today/ The Motley Fool 12/28/2017	Headline: Store Closings: 17 Retailers On The 2018 Death Watch
	Gold Separated From Currency in 1971	Book: Creature From Jekyll Island	Authors: G. Edward Griffin
	Inflation from 1971 to 2017	https://www.officialdata.org/1971-dollars-in-2017?amount=100	Inflation Calculator
	Inflation from 1775 to 1913	Www.businessinsider.com January 6, 2013	Headline: Chart: inflation since 1775 and how it took off in 1933
	Over 50% with government benefits	https://www.forbes.com/ July 2, 2014	Headline: We've Crossed The Tipping Point...
	Housing rising rates	Www.cnbc.com June 23, 2017	Headline: Here's Housing Has Skyrocketed...
	Education rising rates	Www.businessinsider.com July 20, 2015	Headline:...College Tuition Has Skyrocketed Since 1980
	Wage Increases	Www.tradingeconomics.com	United States Wages & Salaries 1960—2018
	Social Security COLA	www.ssa.gov	Social Security Cola History

PAGE #	SUBJECT OR QUOTE	SOURCE	NOTE
	Defined Benefit vs. Defined Contribution Plans	Www. greenbushfinancial.com	Headline: The Shift From Defined Benefit To Defined Contribution Plans
	Life Expectancy	https://www.ssa.gov/planners/lifeexpectancy.html	
	3 In 1 System	Book: Guide To Investing	Author: Robert Kiyosaki
	"If you know your enemy and yourself..."	Google: Sun Tzu Quotes	
	D.I.R.T	Book: Guide To Investing	Author: Robert Kiyosaki
	"Do not dwell in the past..."	Google: Buddha Quotes	
	"Any target attacked..."	Book: 10x	Author: Grant Cardone
	Read, Listen, Associate, Apply	System: Financial Fitness Program	Life Leadership Team
	"A part of all you earn is yours to keep..."	Book: Richest Man In Babylon	Author: George Clason
	Five Tax Advantage Strategies	Book: How To Pay Zero Taxes 2017 Edition	Author: Jeff A. Schnepper
	Withholding Allowances	IRS.gov/IRS	Withholding calculator

PAGE #	SUBJECT OR QUOTE	SOURCE	NOTE
	$1 A Day Doubled Example	Book: Stress Free Retirement	Author: Patrick Kelly
	35% average in debt	Book: BOSS	Author: Ryan and Tyler Thacker
	"Chase Excellence..."	Google: Dr. George Fraser Quotes	
	Five P's Required For Business Development	Book: Built To Last	Author: Jerry L. Porras
	How cars lose value	Www.Trustedchoice.com May 14,2018	Car Depreciation
	Credit Card payment calculation	Www.Bankrate.com	Credit Card Calculator
	Fractional Reserve Banking	Book: Creature From Jekyll Island	Author: G. Edward Griffin
	Small Business Stats, Avg. Income of $46K/year	Quickbooks.Intuit.com, March 13,2015	Info based on 2007 SBA Data
	Insurance is principle	Book: Guide To Investing	Author: Robert Kiyosaki
	3 roles to build a business system	Book: E-Myth	Author: Michael Gerber
	4 rules for building wealth	Book: Unshakable	Author: Tony Robbins

PAGE #	SUBJECT OR QUOTE	SOURCE	NOTE
	Indexed Insurance Products	Book: The Retirement Miracle	Author: Patrick Kelly
	EPS definition, 15 x P/E Average	Google: Investopedia	Headline: The Shift From Defined Benefit To Defined Contribution Plans
	EPS Comparison To Stock Price	Www.quora.com	Headline: What Is A Good EPS Figure For Stock Investing?
	Net income Formula	Google: Investopedia	
	Stocks vs. Bonds	Www.FinancialSumarai.com	
	Real Estate growth	Www.cnbc.com/money, 6-23-2017	Headline: Here's How Much Housing Prices Have Skyrocketed.
	Leading countries who produce/purchase gold	Www.investingnews.com, April 15, 2018	Headline: Largest Producers Of Gold By Country
	Inflation average	Www.usinflationcalculator.com	Headline: Current US Inflation Rates 2008-2018
	Permanent life insurance used by business greats	Book: Money. Wealth. Life Insurance	Author: Jake Thompson
	History of Network Marketing	Www.networkmarkinghq.com	Headline: February 3, 2018
	Network Marketing Growth In Sales	Www.mastermindevent.com	

PAGE #	SUBJECT OR QUOTE	SOURCE	NOTE
	"I'd rather earn 1% of 100 people..."	Google: J. Paul Getty quotes	
	67% of world's population will use mobile phones	Www.venturebeat.com, June 13, 2017	Headline: 5 Billion People Now Have A Mobile Phone Connection
	Elvis Presley Enterprise	https://en.m.wikepedia.org/wiki/elvis_presley_enterprises	
	Gold prices from year 2000 to 2018	Www.onlygold.com	Headline: Historical Spot Gold, Annual High & Low Prices...
	Dynasty started by Mayer Amschel Rothschild	https://en.m.wipedia.org/wiki/rothschild_family	
	Charitable giving	https://givingusa.org/ June 12, 2017	Giving USA 2017: Total Charitable Donations
	95% of Americans are broke	Google: Dept. Of Labor Statistics	
	Distribution Of Book In 1920s	Book: Richest Man In Babylon	Author: George Clason
	Average Market Returns	Www.thebalance.com	Headline: 20 Years of Stock Returns, by Calendar Year, june 23, 2018
	Cultivate Empowerment Atmosphere	Book: Powernomics	Author: Dr. Claud Anderson
	"If you want to build wealth..."	Book: Money, Master The Game	Author: Tony Robbins

PAGE #	SUBJECT OR QUOTE	SOURCE	NOTE
	Own nothing, control everything	Google: Nelson Rockefeller Quotes	
	Law Of The Lid	Book: 21 Irrefutable Laws Of Leadership	Author: John Maxwell
	A Pure Trust...	Www.originalintent.org	Statutory vs. Non-Statutory Trusts
	"A good man leaves an inheritance..."	The Bible—Proverbs 13:22	
	Harvard University Endowment Fund	Www.harvard.edu	About Harvard/ Harvard At A Glance
	"You can have anything..."	Book: Over The Top	Author: Zig Ziglar
	Donald Trump's children worth	Www.cheatsheet.com, May 11, 2018	Headline: How Much The Trump Kids Are Worth...
	"A vision without action..."	Google: Joel A. Barker Quotes	Used regularly by Marlon Smith

About the **AUTHOR**

Rodney D. Archer is the author of TAKE BACK Your Wealth! He is a community organizer of Family Wealth, a financial educator, financial curriculum writer, a national speaker and financial systems architect. Rodney was born and raised in Syracuse, NY. He attended Auburn University for Architecture, was in retail management for 14 years and entered the financial services industry as a life and health insurance agent in 2005. He entered the mortgage industry in 2006, then became a financial wellness coach in 2010 and a wealth strategist in 2016. He is a Certified Financial Education Instructor from the National Financial Education Council and is Board of Director Chairman for some business clients and President of Arrow Financial Services USA, Inc., The Acceleration Group, LLC and Dominion Partners Inc. All companies are centered around financial services.

Members of the
FAMILY WEALTH COMMUNITY

Shaughn Lee & Aviance lives in Charlotte, NC and have two twin boys. Shaughn Lee is a systems engineer and Aviance works in the healthcare profession. Shaughn Lee is also a Wealth Strategist with Family Wealth.

Members of the
FAMILY WEALTH COMMUNITY

Demond Raybon is the CEO and co-founder of StealthEnomics. He has a team of 8 staff and 4 partners helping him build a business to scale and to last. Demond is a Business Strategist with Family Wealth.

Kimbell and Nicole Collins are from Austin, Texas. Kimbell works as a Project Manager Engineer and Nicole works as a Nurse in healthcare profession. They have one son together. Kimbell is a licensed Real Estate Agent and Wealth Strategist with Family Wealth.

Pastor Sean and Lady Kim Weaver are former pastors of True Destiny Church and are building Wealth Building Centers nationwide. They have four children. Pastor Sean is a Wealth Ambassador & Strategist with Family Wealth.

www.ingramcontent.com/pod-product-compliance
Lightning Source LLC
Chambersburg PA
CBHW051124160426
43195CB00014B/2327